YALE NEW CLASSICS

VIRGIL'S
GEORGICS

A NEW VERSE TRANSLATION BY
JANET LEMBKE

YALE UNIVERSITY PRESS   NEW HAVEN AND LONDON

Published with assistance from the Kingsley Trust
Association Publication Fund established by the Scroll
and Key Society of Yale College.

Designed by Sonia Shannon.
Set in Galliard type with Trajan display by Integrated
Publishing Solutions, Grand Rapids, Michigan.
Printed in the United States of America by Edwards
Brothers, Ann Arbor, Michigan.

Library of Congress Cataloging-in-Publication Data
Virgil.
[Georgica. English]
Virgil's Georgics : a new verse translation / by Janet Lembke.
p.   cm.
Includes bibliographical references.
ISBN 0-300-10792-7 (alk. paper)
1. Didactic poetry, Latin—Translations into English.
2. Agriculture—Poetry.   I. Title: Georgics.   II. Lembke,
Janet.   III. Title.
PA6807.G4L46   2005
873'.01—dc22
2004024962

A catalogue record for this book is available from the
British Library.

The paper in this book meets the guidelines for permanence
and durability of the Committee on Production Guidelines
for Book Longevity of the Council on Library Resources.

10 9 8 7 6 5 4 3 2 1

In memory of

J O H N   H E R I N G T O N

who first suggested, decades ago, that I translate Virgil's *Georgics*

CONTENTS

TRANSLATOR'S NOTE

For me, the best way to understand work written in Latin or Greek is to move inside the lines as if they constitute a dwelling and to make myself at ease in its many rooms. From beginning to end, abiding within Virgil's *Georgics* has been a joy. In one small but important sense, I have made this translation in homage to my father, himself a farmer, who taught me to love cows and vegetable gardening. In a larger sense, it has sprung from responding to the seduction of Virgil's hexameters and his superb use of his native tongue. There's a challenge here, too—doing justice to his lines in a language he could not have imagined.

But the poem was written two millennia ago. The practices it recounts, the tribes and lands it mentions, and its many place-names are foreign indeed, in many cases striking no contemporary resonance. So, in an effort to bridge the gap between then and now, to make the poem more accessible and less remote, I have used the present-day names of some geographic features, like towns, lakes, and rivers. The lakes that Virgil calls Larus and Benacus are translated, for example, as Como and Garda, respectively. The land of Mysia is placed in its modern location, Anatolia. I have also taken some liberties to help today's reader feel more at home. Virgil's Rhodope, a mountain range in western Thrace, becomes, simply, either Rose Mountain or a Thracian range.

The names of mythical characters have been translated in several ways. Well-known figures—Arethusa the nymph, Aristaeus the beekeeper, and Silvanus the Roman god of woodlands, for example—retain their names. Other names have been omitted entirely, like those of Titans and monsters, which would have created pictures in the Roman mind; instead, a picture in English is given: the Titan Iapetus becomes "one who fathered Atlas," the monster Typhoeus "one with snake-fingered hands." The names of the many nymphs attending Cyrene in book IV have been transformed to rough English equivalents; Drymo, Xantho, Ligea, and Phyllodoce become Woods Girl, Golden, Clear Voice, and Fancy Leaf. Still other names are retained but given adjectives according to their meaning: "gray-green Glaucus, all-seeing Panopea."

Throughout the poem, I have generally been able to find English that matches Virgil's Latin line for line. The line numbers given in this English version are congruous with those found in the Latin text. The text used is that meticulously edited and annotated by Richard F. Thomas (Cambridge, 1988).

The few currently easy-to-come-by translations of the *Georgics,* from John Dryden's to those of C. Day Lewis (Oxford, 1940) and L. P. Wilkin-son (Penguin, 1982), have been rendered in British English by men who know much about poetry but little about farming. My pleasure has been to use American English. In with grain, out with corn! Out with trun-cheons and buskins, in with sturdy twigs and boots!

Several people merit gratitude. Debra Schrishuhn, who breeds Egyp-tian Arabian horses, made sure I used modern horse terms to translate Virgil's descriptions. Where he used *alta,* which might well be translated as "high," to characterize a noble neck, I use instead "arched," for a neck that's "high" is nowadays seen as a fault. My veterinarian daughter, Lisa Lembke, provided much information on sheep and goats. And Sara Mack, a fine Latinist, read through my drafts and came up with excellent suggestions, many of which I have adopted. To all of you, my heartfelt thanks. Thanks go, as well, to the National Endowment for the Arts, which provided a generous fellowship to support this translation.

Last but not least, a ghost is to be credited. S. Bess Summerson, my maternal grandmother's sister, died before I was born. But on the flyleaf of a book that I treasure she signed her name and wrote the date, October 19,

1894. The book's full title spills down the entire page, but the first part will suffice: *Mitchell's Ancient Atlas, Containing Maps Illustrating Classical and Sacred Geography* by S. Augustus Mitchell and published in Philadelphia by E. H. Butler & Co. I have been able to consult its maps to learn precisely the ancient locations of the many places to which Virgil refers, including Calabria, Thrace, Thessaly, Scythia, and Mysia. I felt my great-aunt's guiding presence as I journeyed between Latin and English.

INTRODUCTION

The *Georgics* is a poem for our time. Though written more than two thousand years ago, it speaks to us just as it spoke to Virgil's contemporaries. The poem not only gave specific instructions to Italian farmers but also passionately advocated caring without cease for the land and for the crops and animals it sustained. A message inhabits the instructions: only at our gravest peril do we fail to husband the resources on which our lives depend. That council is as valid for today and tomorrow as it was for long-gone yesterdays.

Georgics — the word means "farming." The poem is indeed a love song to almost everything that grows or grazes on the land. With a few understandable exceptions, like snakes and grain-plundering mice, plants and animals alike receive Virgil's laud. But, like many lovers, Virgil was also filled with doubts and blamed passion itself for much that may go awry. Despite the best human efforts, the most diligent, unremitting hard work, the world in which we live has never been made perfect. And Virgil's coming of age was filled with dispiriting, chaotic events — widespread political power grabs, corruption, civil wars, assassinations — which he was helpless to counter except in the singing of his poems.

Publius Vergilius Naso was born on October 15, 70 B.C., in Andes, a rural hamlet near Mantua in Cisalpine Gaul, now known as Lombardy. His parents, people of respectable means, came from peasant stock and were farmers. Virgil was thus well acquainted with earth, farm animals, and crops from his earliest days. Educated first in Mantua, Cremona, and

Milan, he went south to Rome at the age of seventeen and not long thereafter to Naples, where he lived for much of the rest of his life. His studies, which included Latin, Greek, rhetoric, and mathematics, were precisely those that would appeal to any young man enamored of words and the music they make. His broad command of Latin and Greek literature, both poetry and prose, is documented by his poems, which refer to, translate, incorporate, and conflate lines and ideas from an amazing range of literary treasures. He was intimately acquainted with the work of his literary predecessors, from Homer and Hesiod, Greek epic poets who flourished about 800 B.C., to Roman writers, including not only poets, playwrights, and orators but also Marcus Porcius Cato (234–149 B.C.) and Marcus Terentius Varro (116–27 B.C.), both of whom wrote in prose on matters pertaining to farming.

Why write on farming? To understand Virgil's probable motives in composing a long poem on that subject, it's necessary to look more closely at the times in which he lived. For more than a century before he was born, the Roman Republic, founded in the eighth century B.C., had been moribund, and when Virgil arrived in the world it had entered its drawn-out death throes. Power struggle followed on power struggle for control of the state as the conservative, anciently empowered aristocrats of the Senate waged political and civil wars with the nouveau-riche knightly class made wealthy by trade, agribusiness, and war. Roman expansion throughout the Mediterranean was a prime cause of governmental instability, for the entrenched senatorial class found itself unable to deal with the concomitant economic, social, and military problems. The citizen-soldier of the Republic, loyal to the state, was being shoved aside by the professional, faithful not to the state but to commander, cohort, and the opportunities for plunder. By the end of the second century B.C., the army had become a war machine. The issues of the day included extending citizenship to all of Italy's inhabitants, redistributing land to small farmers, and providing cheap grain for the lowest classes, whose numbers had been dramatically increased by landless veterans and dispossessed peasants. The city of Rome suffered from a dangerous urban bloat.

Even those who are now distant from the study of ancient history will remember many of the names of the belligerents. Though members of an aristocratic clan, the statesmen Tiberius and Gaius Gracchus worked for agrarian reform in the last third of the second century B.C. In 132 B.C., Tiberius was murdered by men who supported the Senate; in 121, his brother, in imminent danger of being overthrown, committed suicide. Slightly later, the reformer Marius (155–86 B.C.) and the conservative Sulla (138–78 B.C.) fought bloody battles. Not long after, the Social War raged from 90 to 89 B.C., when Rome's allies in both northern and southern Italy, demanding compensation for military service, revolted against the capital. After two years of carnage, the war's resolution brought Roman citizenship to more than half a million Italians and gave political unity to the peninsula south of the Po river. But it did not bring an end to bloodshed. And citizenship would not be extended to Italians living north of the Po for another forty years; it came in 49 B.C., the year Virgil turned twenty-one.

One of the next convulsions occurred when Julius Caesar (100?–44 B.C.) and the aristocrat Pompey (106–48 B.C.), though allied by politics and marriage, waged a protracted civil war in the middle years of the first century. Who should be consul and thus rule over Rome? Only blood could decide. In 49 B.C. (the year Virgil became a citizen), Caesar, who had consolidated control over Gaul, famously led his army across the Rubicon, a small stream separating Cisalpine Gaul from Italy proper. It was a hasty march home meant to bring a halt to what he regarded as Pompey's usurpation of power. By reentering Italy with his troops, he broke the law forbidding a general to lead his soldiers out of the province to which he had been assigned. "Crossing the Rubicon" now means "taking irreversible steps." After three years of internecine fighting not just on Italian soil but also in Spain, Greece, Numidia, and Egypt, Caesar prevailed, assuming the dictatorship in 46 B.C. At that time, it was clear that he who commanded the army commanded all power. But two years later Caesar was killed by Cassius, Brutus, and their coconspirators, who hoped to restore the Republic. In the subsequent squabbling, Cassius

and Brutus busied themselves carving up Roman territories, including
Macedonia and Syria. Both were defeated in 42 B.C. by Mark Antony
(82/81–30 B.C.) and Caesar's great-nephew Gaius Octavius (63 B.C.–A.D.
14) at the battle of Philippi on the west coast of Greece. On Caesar's
death, Mark Antony had nominated himself Caesar's successor. Caesar's
will, however, had named his great-nephew as his heir and specified that
his name be changed to Octavian. The civil wars finally ended in 31 B.C.,
when Virgil was thirty-nine years old. The end was occasioned by Octa-
vian's decisive defeat of Antony in a naval battle at Actium in north-
western Greece. Although a pro forma empire had existed at least since
the second-century days of Marius and Sulla, this form of government
was given official recognition in 23 B.C., with Octavian, now known as
Augustus Caesar, as its nominal founder. For the first time in more than
two hundred years, peace settled on the land.

What does all this have to do with farming? A great deal. The sim-
plest reason that Virgil chose such a subject is, of course, that he bore a
love for the land deep in his very marrow — he had been born to it. His
Georgics is also an act of homage to Hesiod. But more important, he
understood what happened to the land when smallholders were dispos-
sessed. People went hungry when it became an unproductive kingdom
of weeds. Along with many others, his own family is said to have lost its
acreage near Mantua when the property was awarded in 42 B.C., after the
battle of Philippi, as compensation to some of Antony's veterans; Virgil
supposedly regained it through the influence of acquaintances who were
well connected to Octavian. Even if this story is not true, Virgil certainly
knew farm families who had been made landless and homeless. The *Geor-
gics,* ignited by deeply felt personal experience, is in many respects a
heartfelt cry for homecoming, for returning landholders and their fami-
lies to the fields and pastures they had lost through no fault of their own.
The poem is not in any sense, however, a political polemic, designed to
sway opinion and bring about the repopulation of rural Italy. But it may
well provoke a contemporary reader to think wistfully of the disappear-

ance of family farms across North America, though the reasons are far different from those of Virgil's day.

From early on, Virgil was supported in his work by patrons. The first was Asinius Pollio (76 B.C.–A.D. 4), Mark Antony's man, who assumed a neutral political position after Antony's suicide in 30 B.C. Maecenas (70–8 B.C.), a wealthy diplomat and one of Octavian's chief ministers, was the second. Virgil dedicated the *Georgics* to him by name in each of the poem's four books.

The *Georgics* is quadripartite, comprising four books, each of which is devoted to a particular aspect of agriculture. Book I deals with field crops, the astronomical signs that tell the farmer when to sow and when to harvest, and the implements needed to work the land. The theme of book II is trees and vines. Line 266 brings a fine piece of information: the original meaning of the phrase "grape arbor," which is commonly thought of today as a latticework trellis or a post-and-wire fence on which grapevines may climb. The first support for a grapevine, however, was a tree (usually elm or oak), for which the Latin word is *arbor.* Book III treats of livestock, mainly cattle and horses, sheep and goats. Bees buzz and swarm throughout book IV, which also includes an epyllion, a mini-epic, which tells the tale of the world's first beekeeper, Aristaeus, who lost his bees and then, in wondrous fashion, recovered them. Orpheus, Eurydice, and infinitely changeable Proteus figure in the farmer's quest.

The central thesis of the *Georgics* is that labor — sheer, ceaseless hard work — is the only barrier between the farmer and ruin. All too often, it's a flimsy one. Storms strike, drought bakes the land, insects infest the granaries, weeds ensnarl the fields, disease fells flocks and herds wholesale, and nothing the farmer does — not hoeing with extra diligence, not saying prayers over and again — can keep the random blows of nature from wrecking his enterprises. The last 150 lines of book III show this bleak view: snakes threaten not just cattle but people too; incurable infections kill the sheep; no life is safe. Virgil also writes there of a mythic bygone day in which all the domestic and some wild animals were wiped by disease from the face of the earth. The catastrophes of the time are exemplified in book III.515–19:

> But look, the ox, smoking under the heavy plowshare,
> collapses and vomits blood mixed with foam from his mouth
> and groans in his extremity. The sorrowing
> plowman goes, unyoking the ox that mourns its brother's death,
> and in the midst of the job leaves the plow idle.

And the newly unyoked ox wanders off toward its own death. Even the goddess Juno can find no cattle for her rites, and worshipers ride to her temple in chariots drawn by mismatched oxen. Despairing views like these are not uncommon in the poem, and they may be fairly interpreted as reflections of the troubled times in which the poet lived and of his trepidation that the peace achieved by Octavian was frangible.

An underlying thesis of the *Georgics* is that agriculture is the underpinning of civilization and the existence of civil communities. Virgil refers often in the poem to the age of Saturn, its overthrow by Jupiter, and the new era that ensued. The picture of Saturnian life that he presents is akin to that of the Big Rock Candy Mountain, with its cigarette trees and lemonade springs, all growing without human labor, all free for the taking. Italy in the day of Saturn was a land of milk and honey. But when Jupiter vanquished the old order, it became necessary for humankind to labor for a living. Fields required tilling, animals, training and pasturage, and they still do. From that time on, we have no longer had access to innocent leisure. In one crucial sense, although it is a sense of which Virgil would have been unaware, the change from the golden age to one of labor was real. And it occurred when humanity hauled itself out of its biologically ordained hunting-gathering niche by domesticating plants and animals. With that rapid and wrenching event, which took place some twelve to fourteen thousand years ago, certain hitherto unthinkable phenomena transformed human existence. Because people were able to stay put, settlements became possible, and growing urban agglomerations led to the many miseries of city life, from noise to crowded slums. When the cooperation necessary in tiny, tribal communities was lost, hierarchies developed, with a rich and powerful few at the top and masses of serfs and slaves at the bottom. War became a way of life, either to protect one's possessions or to gain more at the expense of others, be they neighbors or distant foes. In his nostalgia for the lost golden age, Virgil shows an intuitive grasp of the havoc wrought in human life by urbanization and warfare, which appeared — and still appears — to be unending.

But joy and gentleness suffuse the poem as much sorrow and gloom. Virgil writes tenderly of wintertime work in the farmer's household (book 1.291–96):

I know a man, too, who stays awake by the last light
of a winter fire and carves points on torch-stakes with a sharp
   knife,
while his wife, lightening her eternal work with song,
runs her lively shuttle through the loom's warp threads
or cooks down the sweet must of new wine over the fire, using
leaves to skim off the foam in the simmering copper kettle.

And this passage paints a lyric picture of rural life (book III.322–30):

But, when joyful summer at the West Wind's bidding sends
both sheep and goats into the woods, into the pastures,
let us go to the chilly fields as the Morning Star
rises, while the day is new, while the grass still glistens
and the dew on its green blades most appeals to the cattle.
Then, when the fourth hour of heaven builds dryness and thirst
and the arbors erupt with the song of complaining cicadas,
I shall bid the flocks beside wells and deep standing pools
to drink the water that burbles down into oaken troughs.

Like these passages, the whole of the *Georgics* is filled with rural images that attest to Virgil's close observation. Delighting in detail, he is able to make the reader feel the early morning chill and elsewhere in the poem catch the fragrance of thyme. Not surprisingly, many of his bits of advice about matters agricultural are valid today. We use the same rakes, hoes, pruning tools, baskets, and pails. We use the same methods for grafting. We still test soil by squeezing it: loam hardly crumbles when it's kneaded and can't be formed into a ball, while a heavy, clayey soil will be compacted.

An eminent Virgilian scholar has assured me that "Virgil never had fun," but many passages in the *Georgics* belie that dour opinion. The opening lines of book II are a fine example of the poet at play: he issues an almost impudent invitation to the "Father of Wine-Making," Bacchus, to tug off his boots, join the poet in the vat to stomp grapes, and dye his bare legs purple in the juice. Book II's delicious descriptions of a sampling of grapes and wines may well indicate that Virgil was a seriously appreciative lover of wine.

The poem is also rich with praise — praise for the accomplishments and conquests of Caesar, as Virgil styles Octavian throughout the poem, and praise for Italy. No land on earth, not Persia or India or the Afghans' land, can equal Italy's glories. Though he had not seen them at first hand, Virgil's knowledge of other lands and other ways of life was almost encyclopedic; the poem abounds in references to countries like Scythia and Parthia as well as to the lifeways of their inhabitants and to geographic features like the Black Sea and Caucasian mountain ranges. But unlike these far-flung venues, glorious Italy is abundant in crops, wine-producing grapes, olives, and fattened herds. The countryside is free of predatory tigers and lions. Great cities, "jewels of human effort" (book II.155), have been built, as have hillside towns that overlook purling rivers. Indulging in shameless hyperbole, Virgil writes (book II.149–50),

Spring is eternal here, and summer lasts more than three months.
Twice a year, the cows bear calves, twice the trees yield fruit.

The full-hearted burden of the whole song is Virgil's love for his native land.

To our great good fortune, three long poems by Virgil survive. The earliest is the *Eclogues,* sometimes called the *Bucolics,* comprising ten poems on pastoral subjects; they were composed between 42 and 37 B.C. The model is the idylls of Theocritus, who flourished about 280 B.C. in Alexandria at the court of Ptolemy, but Virgil has brought distinctive touches to the pastoral mode. Some of the *Eclogues* are true to the model, in which herdsmen laud their simple rural lives. But others refer clearly to the world Virgil knew by heart, for the first and ninth despair over the dispossession of shepherds of their pastures, and the fifth, lamenting the death of Daphnis, the king of the shepherds, may be read as a poem on the recent death of Julius Caesar. One shepherd, Tityrus, appears in both the *Eclogues* and the *Georgics;* we meet him in the first line of the first eclogue as he sprawls under the crown of a spreading beech and, in the *Georgics'* last line, encounter him again prostrate on the ground under the very same tree.

The *Eclogues* were followed by the *Georgics,* written between 37 and 30 B.C., as the seemingly endless civil wars finally came to an end. The models for the *Georgics* are many and varied. Chief among them is Hesiod's *Works and Days,* composed during or slightly after Homeric times. Didactic in nature, it posits a golden age superseded by other ages, in which Zeus commands men to work hard and ceaselessly. A third of the *Works and Days* deals with the farmer's year, especially with astronomical signs and the growing of grain. The *Georgics* goes further, undertaking to instruct farmers not only in these matters but also in many others, among them seasonal tasks, making implements, planting crops and vineyards, harvesting, breeding and training animals, and keeping bees. Like Hesiod's poem, the *Georgics* posits a golden age that was superseded by an era characterized by *labor* — no-nonsense hard work. But Virgil, skeptical about the usefulness of reverence and prayer, does not try to promulgate Hesiod's strict piety. Rather, he doubts the ability of piety to prevent ruin. He does, however, follow Hesiod in the insistence on the farmer's moral obligation to work, work, and never stop working. Virgil describes his own work this way (book II.176): "I sing Hesiod's song through the Roman towns."

Several other Greek poets also influenced Virgil. One was Pindar (518/522–ca. 438 B.C.), who wrote elaborate odes to celebrate victories in the great athletic games. He is Virgil's probable source of the myth detailing Cyrene's seduction by Apollo and the subsequent birth of Aristaeus; in addition, he began many of his odes by erecting a splendid building from which the body of the poem proceeds. Virgil paid homage to this trope with the temple he builds for Caesar in the proem to book III. Another influential poet was Callimachus, a North African of Greek descent who flourished about 270 B.C. in the literary and courtly circles of Ptolemaic Alexandria. Callimachus's contribution to Virgil and his contemporaries, Horace for one, was a stylistic ease that did not pontificate or pay dull, imitative tribute to masterworks but rather contained elegantly sophisticated diction and allusions that added body to the ideas expressed. Some of Callimachus's hymns and epigrams as well as numerous fragments are available today. A poet on whom Virgil drew for subject matter rather than style was Aratus (ca. 315–ca. 245 B.C.), a Macedonian Greek, author of *Phaenomena,* a poem concerned with astronomy and weather signs. It was a rendering into verse of a prose treatise that had appeared a century earlier. Widely translated into Latin, it still exists. Two now-lost works by the minor poet Nicander (probably second century) — one on farming, the other on bees — may also have contributed to Virgil's store of information on those subjects, but all that's now left of Nicander's writing are lines outlining antidotes to poison and remedies for bites.

One poet composing in Latin was certainly the most inspirational of all: Lucretius, who flourished in Virgil's century, the first century B.C., and wrote *De rerum natura,* "On the Nature of Things," a poem converting the rather dry philosophy of Epicurus (341–270 B.C.) into lively dactylic hexameters. Virgil, who first read the poem while in his mid-teens, knew it well and in fact in his late teens joined an Epicurean community in Naples (which Virgil was wont to call Parthenope after its tutelary nymph). Lucretius's poem treats of such topics as physics and atomic theory, friendship as the most useful expression of human interaction, and the equation of good with pleasure, although not in an eat-drink-and-be-merry sense. The greatest good is the absence of pain. Lucretius also posited several ages of humankind, the latest of which occurred when kings started founding cities and divided up herds and lands. (Lucretius seems to have had a grasp on the vicissitudes created by urbanization and private ownership.) The most significant effect of Lucretius's long poem on Virgil's writing may have been the elder poet's vivid imagery. The pictures of natural phenomena and human activities are immensely lively, illustrating everything from weather, earthquakes, volcanic eruptions, and the summer flooding of the Nile to hunting parties and seduction in the woods. The big lesson Virgil learned may well have been that didactic poetry is more than a matter of telling people what to do—it must also show them how to do it.

Virgil had access to a world of prose as well as poetry. His fellow Romans Cato and Varro have been mentioned. Cato's book, which appeared about 160 B.C., is *De agricultura*, "On Agriculture"; that of Varro, Virgil's contemporary and proprietor of a considerable estate, *Res rustica*, "Rural Topics." In his nineties when he wrote his book, Varro apparently intended to leave instructions on farm management for his wife. Virgil happily appropriated passages and transformed them into hexameters. An example occurs in the *Georgics*, book III.322–38, a passage in which Varro's description of the herdsman's tasks from dawn to dusk in the summer pasturage of sheep and goats is turned into lines lyric in their beauty. Another, older source of biological fact and rumor is the Greek scientist Aristotle (384–322 B.C.).

Virgil's poetic career culminated in the writing of the *Aeneid*, a fulfillment of his ambition, stated in the sixth *Eclogue*, to compose an epic. The *Aeneid*, which commanded the last eleven years of the poet's life, tells the story of Rome's god-ordained founding by Aeneas, a survivor of the Trojan War. It is an intensely patriotic poem that treats not only of legend but also of individuals, their stories and emotions, including Aeneas's exile from his native land and his passionate love affair with the Carthaginian queen Dido, who represents, in an entirely human fashion, the threats to Rome of non-Roman ways of life. To gain a better knowledge of the time that Aeneas had spent in Greek territory, Virgil traveled to Greece in 19 B.C., fell ill there, and returned to Brundisium (modern Brindisi) in Calabria, which then was the heel of Italy's boot on the Adriatic Sea. There he died, leaving the *Aeneid* unfinished with instructions that it be destroyed. To the great benefit of posterity, it was not.

The inscription on his tomb in Naples tells all that he felt important for us to know:

Mantua me genuit, Calabri rapuere, tenet nunc
Parthenope; cecini pascua, rura, duces.
[Mantua bore me, Calabria seized me, now Naples
holds me; I have sung pastures, farms, leaders.]

VIRGIL'S
GEORGICS

BOOK ONE

What makes the crops rejoice, Maecenas, under what stars
to plow and marry the vines to their arbor of elms,
what care the cattle need, what tending the flocks must have,
how much practical knowledge to keep frugal bees —
here I start my song. You, brightest luminaries of sky's   5
vast world who lead the onrolling year through the heavens,
you, old Planter God, and you, generous Ceres, if earth
by your gift exchanged wild acorns for plump grains of wheat
and mingled ancient river water with her first-ever grapes;
and you, guardian Gods of Fields and Folds, always present   10
in the countryside (step lightly, dance, Gods and Tree Nymphs!):
I sing your gifts. And you, Neptune, for whom Earth, struck
by your forceful trident, poured out the first whickering horse;
and you, spirit that dwells in all groves, for whom three hundred
snow-white steers crop bramble-thickets in the Cyclades;   15
and you, Pan, protector of sheep, Arcadia's lord. Leaving
native groves and the woods on your holy mountain, may you come,
caring, here as you care for your peaks at home; come, Minerva,
creator of olives; you, too, young man, who showed farmers
the plow; and you, Silvanus, holding an uprooted cypress;   20
and every god and goddess, defending our fields with good will,
both you who nurture fruits that volunteer unsown
and you who send seedlings ample rain from heaven.

You equally, Caesar, though we don't yet know which cohort
of the gods will soon enroll you — whether you'll wish to keep   25
cities safe and care for our lands, so the great circling world will
take you as source of earth's fruits and master of seasons,
placing Venus' wreath of myrtle around your temples;
whether you shall come as god of the vast sea, and sailors worship
only your holy spirit, Ultima Thule bow down to you,   30
and Ocean's wife spend every wave to buy you for her daughter;
whether you shall add yourself to the long summer months as
a new star in the place that has opened mid Virgo
and the clutching Claws (fiery Scorpio himself has now pulled back
his arms and left you more than a fair share of heaven):   35
whatever you shall be (Hell does not hope for you as king,
nor may such ominous passion to rule overwhelm you,
although Greeks admire the Elysian fields and Proserpina,
called back, does not take the trouble to follow her mother),
grant me smooth passage, assent to this work boldly begun,   40
and with me feel compassion for country people unaware
of their way. Enter and promise even now to hear our prayers.

    At spring's beginning, when ice-cold meltwater runs down
from the mountains and loose clods crumble under the West Wind,
that soon, I'd have my ox groan as he pulls the plow deep   45
and my plowshare glisten, polished by the furrow.
That soil responds to the eager farmer's prayers
only after it has twice felt the sun and twice the cold;
from it, grain spilling over has burst the granaries.
And first, before our plows break open unfamiliar ground,   50
it's wise to learn about the winds and heaven's changing moods,
the condition of the land and its requisite tillage,
and what each tract will bear, what each will reject.
Here grain, there grapes will come most readily to ripening,
and elsewhere saplings and grasses grow green of their own   55

accord. Don't you see that Asia Minor sends saffron perfume,
India ivory, the soft Arabians frankincense, but
naked tribes near the Black Sea send steel, the Sea itself stinking
beaver oil, Epirus the Olympian prizes of her mares?
Nature imposed these laws and everlasting covenants 60
on certain places from the time that Prometheus's son
hurled stones into the empty world, so generating
men, a rude but hardy species. Come then, where the earth
is rich, let your strong oxen deep-plow it in the year's
early months, and with the clods lying exposed, let 65
dusty summer bake them under its powerful suns.
But if the land should prove unfruitful, it will be enough
to build it up with light furrows when Arcturus rises —
there, so that weeds won't smother the crops; here, so that scanty
moisture does not evaporate from unproductive sands. 70

Every other year, let your fields lie fallow after harvest;
likewise allow idle land to keep its stiff, dry stalks.
Or, the stars having changed, you'll sow grains of light red wheat
where, first, you've removed the bean that abounds in rattling pods
or the fruits of the trifling vetch and the breakable 75
stalks and rustling foliage of the inedible pulse.
For, a crop of flax dries up a field, oats dry it up,
as do poppies, suffused with forgetful sleep.
But with crop rotation, work is easy, nor need you feel
shame in saturating parched soil with rich manure 80
and strewing sooty ashes over exhausted land.
So, too, with alternating crops, the fields may rest,
nor is gratitude lacking in the unplowed earth.
Often, it's beneficial as well to set barren fields
on fire and burn the dry stalks with crackling flames. 85
From this, the earth may take in hidden strengths and rich
nutrients, or every imperfection may boil away

in the hot fire and useless moisture be sweated out,
or, heat may open up new pathways and concealed
air holes, through which the sap will rise in sprouting grain,   90
or it may rather harden the earth and shrink its gaping veins
lest soaking rains erode it or the cruel sun's burning
forces blast it, or the North Wind's bone-piercing cold.
He does much who hoes the inert clods and drags harrows
over them — his fields rejoice, nor does golden Ceres   95
observe him in vain from Olympus' royal heights;
he, too, who plows again at right angles with his curved share
through the ridges that he'd cut first across the level ground,
quick to work the land and keep his fields under control.

   Farmers, pray for wet summers and winters with clear blue
      skies.   100
Wheat rejoices most in winter dust; fields, too, rejoice;
Anatolia's Aegean coast prides itself on lack
of cultivation; mountains inland admire their own harvests.
Need I mention him who, having sown the seed, tends the
      fields
hands on and vigorously levels piles of barren sand,   105
then diverts rivulets of running water to his crops
and, when the soil dries up, its sprouted grain burnt, in
      summer's heat —
behold! — brings water from the ridge through irrigation
channels? Falling, it rushes down the smooth stones with a
      hoarse
white noise and restores the thirsty soil with its bubbling jet.   110
And mention him who, lest his grain bend low with heavy ears,
chops down a bountiful wheat crop when the young stalks
of standing grain reach the tops of their furrows, and him
who drains collected moisture from a swamp with thirsty sand,
especially in unsettled weather, if a river swells   115

to overflowing and everywhere spreads a coating of mud
that makes the drainage ditches sweat a thin, damp mist?

Even so, after the hard work of man and ox to turn
earth over, nothing stops the goose bold to uproot wheat,
Eurasian cranes, and chicory with its bitter roots,   120
nor is heavy shade harmless. The Father himself hardly
willed that agriculture would be easy when he called forth
the field with his art, whetting human minds with worries,
not letting his kingdom slip into full-blown laziness.
Before Jove took power, no settlers broke the fields with their
   plows: 125
it was impious then to mark off the land and divide it
with boundaries; people sought land in common, and Earth
   herself
gave everything more freely when no one made demands.
It was Jove who put deadly venom in the hissing snake,
ordered the wolf to turn predator and the deep sea to surge,   130
shook all the honey from the leaves, extinguished fire,
and everywhere held back the wine that flowed fast in the streams
so that, using their brains, men might gradually hammer out
many skills, like searching for stalks of wheat by plowing,
and so that they might strike the spark held in veins of flint.   135
Then rivers first sensed boats of hollowed elder wood;
then the seaman counted and named the stars — Pleiades,
Hyades, the princess whom Jove turned into the bright Bear;
then they learned how to catch game in snares, how to use
   birdlime
and surround vast woodlands with deer dogs and bear dogs;   140
while one man flogs a wide stream with his cast-net seeking
the bottom, another pulls his sodden draglines through the sea;
then came iron's hardness and the grating blade of the saw
(for early men split wood along the grain with wedges);

then came the arts in many guises. Relentless work conquered   145
all difficulties — work and urgent need when times were hard.

　　Ceres first arranged for mortal men to turn the earth
with iron at the time that acorns and arbutus berries
failed in the sacred woods and holy oak groves supplied no food.
Soon, though, blight and weeds attacked the wheat — foul molds   150
infected the stalks, and the useless thistle sent shock troops
into the fields; the standing wheat dies, a rude forest of burs
and puncture vines springs up, poisonous darnel and
sterile wild oats lord it over the once healthy furrows.
So, unless you pursue the weeds with a relentless hoe,   155
scare off the birds with shouting, remove the shade from over-
shadowed farmland with a pruning hook, and call down rain with
　　prayers,
in vain, alas, you'll stare at someone else's heaps of grain
and relieve your own hunger by shaking oak trees in the woods.

　　And I must speak of militant farmers' weapons,   160
without which the crops could not be sown nor sprouted:
first, the plow and the curved share's heavy hardwood frame.
The grain carts of Ceres rolling slowly on the farms,
sledges and drags to smooth the soil, and hoes of unkind heft;
Greek wickerware, as well, and plain farming tools, arbutus-   165
wood hurdles and the winnow used in Bacchus' secret rites.
All of these, acting with foresight, you'll put in and store
if the glory proper to a god-blessed farm is to stay yours.
For your plow, a living elm bent by force in the woods
is tamed into its stock and accepts the curved share.   170
To its stem a shaft extending eight feet is fitted,
along with two moldboards and a double-backed beam.
Beforehand, a linden is felled for the yoke, and a tall beech

for the handle, which turns the wheeled chariot's bottom from
   the rear.
Smoke seeks and seasons the green wood suspended over the
   hearth.   175

    I can present you with many old rules of thumb — unless
you'd avoid them, reluctant to know of minor concerns.
First, your threshing floor must be leveled with a long roller
and worked by hand, then made solid with a chalk that holds fast
lest weeds rise rampant and the floor cracks open, gone to dust.   180
Then, sundry plagues will sport with you — often a small mouse
sets up housekeeping underground and builds its granaries,
or moles, their sight stolen, excavate their tunnels and nests;
the toad lurks in holes, and the horde of monsters that scuttle
forth from the earth, and the weevil plunders a heaping store   185
of grain, as does the ant, fearing an indigent old age.
Note, too, when the nut tree in the woods decks itself
with countless flowers and bends sweet-smelling branches:
if nuts abound, grain crops will develop in the same way,
and a grand threshing will take place in grand summer heat.   190
But if heavy shade from leaves overhead is unrestrained,
the stalks on the threshing floor will be rich only in chaff.
I have seen many farmers wet down their seeds
with alkalis and the watery black dregs of olive oil
so that the beans, plumping out their tricky pods, may yield   195
a greater crop and cook more quickly, even over a low fire.
I have seen seeds long gathered and carefully inspected
lose quality if human effort has not sorted out
the largest every year. So, fate decrees that everything
tumble into a worse state and slide swiftly backwards,   200
just as when someone whose oars can hardly force his boat
against the current should happen to relax his pull,
the flow will seize him, pushing him headlong downstream.

Then, too, we must heed the stars — Arcturus, the two
kids held in Auriga's left arm, and radiant Draco —   205
just as they do, bound for home over wind-tossed waters, who risk
the Black Sea and the jaws of the Hellespont's oyster shoals.
When Libra makes equal the waking hours and those of sleep
and divides the world evenly between light and darkness,
keep working your oxen, men, sow barley in the fields   210
until the time that winter's storms send pelting rain.
Then, too, it's time to cover the seeds of flax and Ceres'
poppy with earth and apply yourselves right away to the plow
while day still permits, while the clouds still float on high.
In springtime, sow beans; then, too, the loose furrows accept you,   215
perennial clover, as well as the annual tending of millet,
when shining Taurus with his golden horns opens the year
and the Dog Star sets, yielding to the rising constellation.
But if you work the soil for a harvest of wheat
and robust spelt — and you'd raise only grain —   220
let the Pleiades vanish at dawn and the Cretan star
set, the brightest and largest in fiery Corona,
before you commit to the furrows the seeds they are due
and consign a whole year's hope to unwilling earth.
Many have begun before Maia's setting, but the crop   225
they desired has thwarted them with empty stalks.
But if you'd sow both vetch and humble legumes and not
disdain tending the Egyptian lentil, Boötes,
on setting, will not send you signs that are hard to read.
Begin and keep on sowing till midwinter's frosts.   230

Accordingly, the golden sun governs his orbit, measured
in fixed parts through the Zodiac's twelve constellations.
Five zones form the heavens, of which one is always ruddy
with the coruscating sun, always torrid from his fires.
Around it, at blue sky's farthest ends, two are spun out,   235

one right, one left, both locked in ice and sullen black storms.
Between these and the middle zone, two were granted
as holy gifts to frail humankind, and the sun's path was cut
through both where the twelve signs' slanted ranks might revolve.
Just as the world rises high in the north's Caucasian peaks,   240
so does it drop, sloping downward in the south of Libya.
One pole is always high above us, but the other,
beneath our feet, black Styx observes, and the countless dead.
Above, mighty Draco snakes a course that winds
like a river around and amid the two Bears,   245
the Bears afraid to dive beneath Ocean's surface.
Beneath, so they say, either the dead of night keeps silence
and its spreading darkness grows ever more thick,
or Dawn goes there to bring back the daylight;
when the sun in the east first breathes on us with snorting steeds,   250
there, at dusk, the Evening Star kindles her lights.
Hence, even with fickle skies, we can predict
the weather; hence, the day of harvest and the time to sow,
and when it's fitting to slap the faithless surface
of the sea with oars, or when to launch a fully armed fleet   255
or, at the proper time, fell a pine for ship's timbers.

Not in vain do we observe the signs' setting and rising,
and the year shared equally by four different seasons.
Whenever chilly rains confine the farmer to his house,
he's given time to ready much that would have to be done   260
in haste under fair skies to come. The plowman hammers the hard
tooth of the blunted plow, hollows trees for vats and troughs,
brands his flocks, or reckons his piles of grain.
Others sharpen stakes and props shaped like two-pronged forks
and prepare ties of Umbrian willow for drooping grapevines.   265
Now, without trouble, weave small baskets of briar canes,
now parch grain over the fire, now grind it on a stone.

In fact, even on holy days, the laws of god and men
permit some work. No piety forbids bringing down
irrigation water, fencing in crops with a hedge,   270
setting snares for birds, burning up tangles of briars,
and dipping a bleating flock in a health-promoting stream.
Often, a driver loads the sides of his slow jackass
with oil or abundant fruit and, on return from town,
brings back a chiseled millstone or a lump of black pitch.   275

  The Moon herself has set various days in various order
as propitious for work. Avoid the fifth — then death's pale king
and the Furies were born; then Earth with unholy birth pangs
bore Titans and monsters — one who fathered Atlas, one with snake-
fingered hands, and the brothers who plotted to overthrow
    heaven.   280
Three times they tried to pile Ossa on Pelion, as you know,
and roll leafy Olympus atop Ossa; three times
the Father tore apart that heap of rocks with a thunderbolt.
The seventeenth is propitious for planting the vine,
yoking and breaking in oxen, and adding new threads   285
to the warp. The ninth favors flight, opposes filching.

  Many tasks give themselves better to the cool of night
or when, at day's beginning, Dawn wets the earth with dew.
At night, patient stalks of grain are best cut, and at night,
dry meadow grasses; at night, no want for long-lasting moisture.   290
I know a man, too, who stays awake by the last light
of a winter fire and carves points on torch-stakes with a sharp
    knife,
while his wife, lightening her eternal work with song,
runs her lively shuttle through the loom's warp threads
or cooks down the sweet must of new wine over the fire, using   295
leaves to skim off the foam in the simmering copper kettle.

But Ceres' golden grain is reaped in midday heat,
in midday heat the threshing floor separates dried seed-heads.
Then, plow bare land, sow bare land. Country folk laze in the
    winter.
In cold weather, farmers mainly enjoy their produce   300
and share it together in cheerful company.
Genial winter invites them in and banishes their cares
just as when heavy-laden ships make port
and the cheerful sailors crown the poop decks with wreaths.
Still, that's the time to pluck acorns from the oak trees   305
and bay laurel's berries, olives, too, and blood-red myrtle;
time to set snares for cranes and nets for the stag,
chase down the long-eared hare as well; time to hunt fallow deer
by whirling the flaxen strap of a Balearic slingshot
when snow lies deep, when rivers shove along blocks of ice.   310

        What should I say about autumn's weather and its stars,
and what men must watch for as the day grows shorter
and summer more soft, or when spring rains fall in cloudbursts,
when ranks of grain bristle in the field and when
the seed-heads on their green stalks plump out with milk?   315
Often, when a farmer led his reaper into the golden fields
and was taking barley off its easily broken stalk,
I have seen all the winds rush together in battle,
which everywhere tore heavy grain up from its deepest
roots and forced it skyward; just so, in a black whirlwind,   320
cold, stormy weather routed light chaff and flying stalks.
Often, too, a huge column of water appears in the heavens,
and clouds, massing on high, roll foul weather in
with its black thunderstorms. The sky falls overhead
as flooding rains wash away healthy crops and the work   325
of the oxen. Ditches fill, deep rivers crest with a loud
rush, and the once-calm sea boils up in a foaming surge of fury.

The Father himself in the dark night of thunderheads hurls
his bolts with right hand striking sparks. From that battering,
   great
Earth trembles. Wild animals seek refuge, and fear lays   330
human hearts low throughout the world. He smites down
Mount Athos, a range in Thrace, or Caucasian peaks
with his lightning spear. Wind-force doubles, rain ever thickens
till now the groves, now the shores groan under the hard gale.
Dreading this, pay heed to the heavens' months and stars,   335
noting when the cold planet Saturn withdraws itself,
where Mercury's fire wanders in the rotating sky.
First of all, venerate the gods and thank splendid Ceres
with annual rites of sacrifice on the newly green grass
at the end of the winter when spring shines fair and bright.   340
Then lambs are fat, then wine is smoothest to the palate,
then sleep is sweet and shadows thick in the mountains.
See that every youth in the countryside worships Ceres.
For her wash the honeycomb with milk and mellow wine.
Three times let the auspicious victim circle the new crops   345
while the whole crowd of farmers follows, rejoicing,
and calls out loudly, summoning Ceres into their homes.
Before anyone applies his scythe to the ripened wheat,
his temples crowned with a twisted wreath of oak, let him
dance a jig in Ceres' honor and chant her old songs.   350

    And so that we can learn from known signs about these
    matters —
summer's heat and hard rains and winds that blow in the cold —
the Father himself decreed what the moon warns every month,
by what sign the winds abate, and what frequent sight
makes the farmer keep his cattle closer to the barn.   355
From the start, when the winds rise, either the rolling straits
of the sea begin to surge and a dry cracking is heard

in the high mountains or far-off, wave-pummeled shores are
thrown into confusion and the groves' rustling becomes a roar.
Then, too, the wave does not keep itself from the curved keel,   360
when the terns come back on swift wings from midocean
and bring their shrill cries to the shore, and when sea-coots
play on dry land and the heron deserts its familiar
marshes to beat its feathered oars above the highest clouds.
Often, too, when strong winds impend, you'll see shooting stars   365
fall sudden in the sky with long, fiery tails gleaming white
behind them as they course through the shadows of the night;
often light chaff and falling leaves whirl about or feathers
bob up and down together on the surface of the water.
But when lightning strikes from the region of the harsh North
    Wind, when   370
the houses of the East and West Winds roll with thunder, all
the fields swim in the ditches' overflow, and every sailor
out at sea furls sodden sails. Rain has never come
without warning: when it looms, cranes in the sky's lofty
reaches take flight to deep valleys, and the heifer, rolling   375
her eyes toward heaven, tests the breezes with nostrils flared,
or the chittering swallow swoops gracefully around the ponds
and the frogs in the mud croak their old-as-time complaint.
And often, the ant, treading a narrow path, carries
her eggs from the innermost nest, and a huge rainbow is seen   380
drinking, and a mob of crows, leaving the feeding grounds
in a long column, rises with a rush of flapping wings.
Then, too, sundry seabirds that eye the freshwater pools
in Asian meadows by Anatolia's Swan River,
vying to splash shoulders and backs with much water,   385
now ducking heads in the stream, now running into the waves
and bathing with zest for the fun of it — you may see these things.
Then, the impudent crow calls down rain with a loud caw
and struts, a solitary bird, upon the shore's dry sand.

Even girls, working their spindles at night, are not   390
unaware of a coming storm when they see the oil's flame
gutter in the lamp and a crust of mold grow on its wick.

    No less, after a storm, you may look for sunny days
with clear skies and anticipate them by reliable signs,
for then the stars' edge appears clear and clean to the eye,   395
nor does the Moon rise indebted to her brother's rays,
nor flimsy, fleecelike clouds float across the sky.
Then, kingfishers, beloved by Thetis, do not spread their wings
to the sun's warmth, nor do pigs in their mud wallows
think of flinging small bundles of straw with their snouts.   400
But mists seek the lowlands, and there, on the plain, they cling,
and, observing the sunset from a perch high in the air,
the owl to no purpose hoots her nocturnal cry.
The sea-hawk, once a king, appears in the clear sky,
and his daughter, a small bird, pays for shearing his red hair.   405
Wherever, fleeing him, she cuts through light air with her wings,
look! — hostile, intending harm, the hawk pursues her through
    heaven
with a strident cry; where he takes himself toward heaven,
fleeing him, she hastens to cut through light air with her wings.
Then, with tight throats, the ravens repeat their clear caws three
    or four   410
times, and often in the high perches where they bed down at
    night,
happy with some odd, unaccustomed pleasure, cry
raucously among themselves amid the leaves. They delight,
storms over and gone, to see again their small broods and sweet
    nests.
I hardly believe that their instincts are indeed divinely given   415
or that Fate awarded them greater foreknowledge of things
but rather that when the weather and intermittent spring

rains alter course and Jupiter, soaked by the South Winds,
thickens what was just now thin and makes the thick loose,
the responses of their senses change, and their hearts receive   420
perceptions other than those left when the wind pursued
the clouds — hence that harmony of birdsong in the fields,
cattle lowing happily, and the ravens' guttural exulting.

For a fact, if you're mindful of the swift Sun and the Moon's
phases rolling by in order, never will tomorrow's hour   425
deceive you, nor the still of night take you by ambush.
When the Moon first begins to wax as her fire returns,
if she beholds a black cloud between indistinct horns,
then hard, heavy rains lie in wait for farmer and sailor.
But if she spreads virginal rosiness over her face,   430
there shall be wind; with wind, the golden Moon always blushes.
If at her fourth rising — that's our best authority —
she proceeds bright and clear through the sky, her horns not
    blunted,
all that day and the days descended from it till the month
measures out shall be free from rain and wind, and sailors, safe   435
ashore, unfurl their vows to the sea's gods and goddesses —
gray-green Glaucus, all-seeing Panopea, sweet Melicertes.

The Sun shall also give signs both on rising and on setting
in the waves: signs of true authority come from the Sun,
those brought in the morning and those at the appearance
    of stars.   440
When, hidden by a cloud, he has covered his early rising
with streaks and contracted to the center of his disk,
let thoughts of rain arise, for the South Wind bears down hard
from above, injurious to trees and crops and herds.
Or when at first light his rays, one here, one there, break through   445
a dense cloud-cover or when Dawn rises pale

on leaving her consort's saffron-gold bed — oh! Then the vine's
foliage will hardly protect the ripened grapes from hail
so hard and heavy that it bounces, rattling, on the roof.
This, too: when he sets after crossing the heavens,   450
you'd be well advised to heed him, for often we observe
the changes in the colors that stray across his face.
Dark gray means rain; a fiery glow, the East Wind;
but if the streaks begin to mingle with ruddy fire,
then you'll see all become turbulent with wind and driving   455
rain alike. On this kind of night, let no one persuade me
to sail deep seas or tear my lines away from the land.
But if his orb shines bright when he brings back daylight,
then puts what he brought away, in vain your fear of
    thunderheads,
and you'll note that the woods are stirred by a fresh North Wind. 460
Last, what the late evening conveys, whence the wind that clears
the sky of clouds, what the humid South intends — the sun
shall give you signs. Who dares to say the sun deceives?
And more: he often warns that secret insurrections press close,
that treachery and hidden wars make ready to burst forth.   465
He also, Caesar's life extinguished, took pity on Rome
when he covered his shining face with iron's rusty darkness
and an impious age feared that night would never end.
Yet, in that time, Earth also and the surface of Ocean,
the obscene dogs and rude birds of ill omen all   470
granted signs. How often we have seen pulsing Etna
pour the contents of her ruptured furnaces over the coast
of Sicily, rolling out balls of fire and molten rock!
Germany heard the clash of battle roll throughout the sky;
struck by extraordinary earthquakes, the Alps shuddered.   475
A huge voice that all could hear rang loud through the silent
    groves,
and pallid phantoms in astounding numbers flickered in

the darkness of the night. Flouting nature, cattle spoke!
Streams stood still, fields split open, in the temples ivory statues
all shed mournful tears and bronze images broke out in sweat.   480
In a swirl, the Po, king of rivers, washed out forests
with his raging high waters and bore away over the fields
the cattle, along with their pens. Nor at that same time
did ominous threads cease to appear in the victims' guts
or blood to pour out of wells, and the hill towns to echo   485
through the whole night with the high, drawn-out howling of
   wolves.
Never did more thunderbolts strike earth out of a clear
sky, nor ill-boding comets, blazing, streak by so often.
So, for a second time, Philippi saw Romans in battle
lines join combat between themselves with weapons equal,   490
nor was it found shameful by the gods that Macedonia
and the broad Balkan plains were twice made fertile by our blood.
And a time shall surely come that, in those countries,
the farmer working the soil with his curved plow
shall discover javelins corroded and scabrous with rust   495
or clank on empty helmets with his heavy hoe
and wonder at the huge bones found in uncovered graves.
Gods of my country, homeland gods, Romulus, mother Vesta,
who protect the Tiber's Tuscan source and the young man's hilltop
abode, do not prevent him from succoring an age   500
in ruins. We have atoned long enough with our blood
for Laomedon's false promise to the gods at Troy.
And heaven's courts have slighted you long enough, Caesar,
charging that you concern yourself with human triumphs.
Here the good and evil have changed places: so many   505
wars in the world, so many forms of wickedness, no honor
for the plow, farmers conscripted, the mournful fields untilled,
and curved pruning hooks are beaten into unbending swords.
Here Euphrates, there Germany goes to war; neighboring

cities, flouting the laws they've both agreed on, take up arms;   510
The unholy god of war rages over the whole world,
just as when a chariot bursts out of the starting gates,
gaining speed as it goes, and the driver futilely yanking
the reins is borne willy-nilly by horses out of control.

BOOK TWO

I've sung the green gardens of earth and the stars in heaven.
Now, Bacchus, you are my song and, with you, the trees that stand
thick in the woods and the fruit of the slow-growing olive.
Father of Wine-Making, come! Everything here overflows
with your gifts. For you, the vines are laden in the vineyard,   5
and the vintage foams in full-to-brimming vats.
Come, Father of Wine-Making, tug off your boots, come with me
to stomp the grapes and dye your bare legs purple in the raw juice.

    To begin with, nature is lavish in bringing forth trees.
You can see for yourself that some, no thanks to us, volunteer,   10
spreading far and wide, tenacious in fields and on banks
of meandering streams — bending willow and pliant broom,
poplar and the willow with pale green, silver-frosted leaves.
Others spring up from seed that lies in the ground — towering
chestnut and the woodland oak with huge leaves and edible   15
acorns, and the oak that Greeks think capable of prophecy.
The thickest growth sprouts up from the roots of others,
like cherry and elm; as a sapling, Apollo's bay laurel
also snuggles under the shade of its mighty mother.
From the first, nature granted these arts so that every kind   20
of forest, thicket, and sacred grove would flourish green.
Still other trees are those we come to know by working them.

One man, cutting suckers from the mother, stocking young roots,
plants them in furrows, while another sets them in the field
with stakes split four ways and spikes of sharpened hardwood.   25
Other trees in the woods need to root by layering,
branches bent and pinned to earth so that living shoots spring up.
Still others need not rise from roots; the pruner may cast
treetop cuttings to earth with no doubt that they'll grow.
But cut the trunk of an olive tree — oh, strange to relate —   30
a root will volunteer, thrusting out of the dry wood.
Often the branches of one tree are safely attached
to those of another — look! Apple grafts bearing fruit
on a pear tree, large-pitted cherries turning red on a plum!

   So, you who work the land, learn the right way to grow
      according   35
to genus and tame wild fruits with your cultivation.
Don't let your fields lie fallow. Mountains in Thrace, mountains
nearby — be glad to grow grapes there and clothe them with olives.
And you be with me, Maecenas, my glory, the greater
part of our shared renown, so that I may finish the work   40
begun. Hoist your sails to fly over the salt-sea.
No, I can't hope to embrace the whole world in my verses,
no, not though I had a hundred tongues, a hundred mouths,
and a voice made of iron. Be with me, sail down the coastline —
land lies in sight. Nor shall I hold you back with impromptu   45
songs, untoward wandering, and windy introductions.

   Trees that volunteer, lifting their branches into the light
are barren, it's true, but they spring up abundant and strong,
for they grow in soil fertile by nature. Yet these, too,
if you make grafts or transplant them to deep-dug trenches,   50
will shed their wildness and, tended with due care,
will bend to your bidding with little delay.

With unproductive suckers that shoot up at a tree's
base, the same may be done, if you set them out in cleared fields;
their mother's high, leafy branches will overshadow them   55
if left alone, robbing them of growth and blighting their fruit.
Then, too, a tree that volunteers from seeds cast by the wind
develops slowly, at last giving shade to our grandchildren,
nor do its fruits breed true but forget their fine flavors,
and wild vines bear bunches of sorry grapes fit only for birds.   60
Plainly, everything requires work, every last plant
mustered into furrows and, with great effort, tamed.
Domestic olives grow best from sturdy, rooted twigs,
vines from layering, myrtles from the entire trunk.
Hardwood hazel trees spring up from suckers, and the great ash,   65
the poplar tree that crowned Hercules with shade, and the acorns
from a great oak in northern Greece. So, too, the date palm
    grows tall,
and the fir, yielding planks that will travel oceans stormy and calm.
But the rough-barked arbutus is grafted with a walnut shoot,
and barren sycamores support productive apple boughs,   70
chestnut flowers blossom on a beech, and a mountain ash turns
    white,
candent with pear flowers, while hogs root acorns beneath an elm.

    Nor are methods all the same for grafting slips and buds.
For, when the buds thrust out of the bark and burst
their scaly coverings, we make a mere slit in the heart   75
of a node; here, inserting a bud from another
species, we teach it to grow into the sap-filled rootstock.
But stocks without nodes are cut open, and wedges used
to drive a deep path into dense wood. There slips from a fruitful
tree are set in and bound. In no time at all, a great   80
tree, amazed by unusual leaves and fruit not its own,
tickles the belly of heaven with its laden boughs.

What's more, one genus hardly fits all mighty elms,
all willows, all hackberries, and every last cypress.
Plump olives, too, have more than one variety — testicle-   85
and shuttle-shaped, and a bitter-berried sort that yields fine oil.
So, too, with apple trees and royal orchards, nor are cuttings
alike for Tuscan and Syrian pears and those that fill your hand.
Nor do the same grapes hang heavy on our arbors as those
Lesbos gathers from its boughs for a flowery wine.   90
Red grapes grow in the northern Aegean, pale grapes in Egypt,
one adapted to rich soil, the other to hardscrabble,
and grapes more suited to black raisin wine or delicate white —
either one could make for staggering feet and a slurring tongue;
purple grapes, yellow grapes, and — how shall I praise you? —
    terraced   95
Alpine vineyards. But don't try to rival Campania's cellars.
And Umbria's vines produce a most full-bodied wine,
unsurpassed by Anatolia and lordly Chios;
and the modest wine made from white grapes that no other excels,
for it pours out fluent and ages impeccably.   100
Nor do I ignore you, muscats from Rhodes, fit for gods' palates
and those of men, nor you, native grapes with clusters big as
    breasts.
But of the abounding varieties and their names, there is
no numbering, nor is it worthwhile to grasp at a number.
He who would know this would like to learn as well how many   105
grains of sand the West Wind roils on the Libyan desert
or, when the East Wind falls on ships with gale force,
would count the waves of the Ionian Sea that crash ashore.

    Not all soils are able willy-nilly to grow all plants.
Willows grow by rivers, alders in the muck of swamps,   110
and the barren wild mountain ash on rocky slopes;
shores are happiest with myrtles, but Bacchus' vines

love sunny hillsides, and the yew, the North Wind's freezing cold.
Look! Earth to its farthest reaches tamed by cultivation —
the Arabs' eastern homes, tattooed tribes north of the Caspian.   115
Trees have their allotted habitats. India alone bears black
ebony; frankincense comes only from Arabia.
What shall I tell you about the fragrant gum that seeps
from the bark and the pods of the evergreen acacia?
What to tell of Ethiopia's groves, gleaming white with soft   120
wool, what of the fine silk combed from leaves in China?
Or, nearer the ocean, the banyan jungles that India
supports, that tract at earth's far end where no flight of arrows
can gain the upper air above the canopy?
Mind you, those people aren't slow at handling a quiver.   125
Persia yields the acidic juices and lasting flavor
of the fruitful citrus tree, none other more efficacious —
if ever wicked stepmothers have poisoned the drinking
cups by mixing herbs and harmful spells — none better to bring
immediate help and drive the lethal toxins from the body.   130
The tree itself grows large and much resembles the bay laurel
(and, did it not release its own distinctive scent,
would be a bay). No wind can cause its leaves to fall,
its flower clings fast indeed, and the Persians use it
to sweeten bad breath and treat congestion in the old.   135

But not the groves of Persia, that land of fabled wealth,
not the Ganges nor the Asian river that's muddy with gold
may vie with Italy's excellence, no, not the Afghans' land,
not India nor the fabled place of sand rich with frankincense.
Bulls shooting flames from their nostrils have never plowed   140
our land so that it may be sown with monstrous dragon's teeth,
nor have our fields of grain bristled with soldiers' helmets and
    spears.
Instead, bountiful crops and Campanian wine fulfill

the land; olives possess it, and grass-fattened herds.
Here, the high-stepping warhorse canters over the plain,   145
here, Umbria, your white herds graze, and the bull, grandest
sacrifice, which, bathed frequently in its holy stream,
leads triumphant Romans to the temples of the gods.
Spring is eternal here, and summer lasts more than three months.
Twice a year, the cows bear calves, twice the trees yield fruit.   150
But predatory tigers don't live here, nor stalking
lionkind, and wolfsbane does not fool the sorry soul who picks it,
nor does the scaly viper, winding sinuous upon
the ground, gather itself into a coil and strike.
Add up the many great cities, jewels of human effort,   155
and the many towns built by hand on rocky hillsides
with rivers purling bright below their ancient walls.
Shall I speak of the Adriatic and Tuscan seas that wash
our coasts? Of the abundant lakes? You, Como, the greatest,
and you, Garda, waves building with the surge and rush of the
    sea?   160
Shall I speak of our harbors and Lake Lucrino's breakwater
where Ocean in outrage crashes and roars
and the port's waves resound as the sea is repulsed
and the salt-tide floods into the channels of Averno?
This country presents us with streams of silver in her veins,   165
and copper mines; her rivers carry a flood of gold.
She has borne a sharp kind of man — hill-town guerrillas,
mountain men raised with adversity, fighters with short spears;
hers, too, men skilled in war — the Decii and Marius,
the great Camillus, the Scipios, and you, Caesar, best of all,   170
already victor in remotest Asia, who now
keeps the unwarlike Middle East far from our Roman hills.
Hail, land of Saturn, bountiful mother of grain and fruits,
bountiful in men. For you I set forth a subject that

anciently commanded skill and praise. Daring to tap   175
the sacred springs, I sing Hesiod's song through the Roman
   towns.

   Now the genius of soil claims its place, its vigor and color
and its natural power for supporting plants.
Olives—to begin with, hardscrabble soil and barren hills
of the clayey sort and fields full of stones and scrub,   180
rejoice in a god-given grove of long-lived olives.
In a region like this, wild trees spring up everywhere
and cover the ground with their numberless berries.
But soil that is rich and blessed with hidden moisture
or a plain filled with vegetation and good nutrients   185
(as we see often in a valley cupped by mountains;
here streams tumble down from the rocky cliffs, and their flow
bears alluvial silt) or an upland facing south
that nurtures bracken inimical to the curved plowshare—
this land will one day give you the hardiest vines,   190
yielding a river of Bacchus' delight, and yield bursting grapes,
yield the juice for libations we pour from a golden cup
when the well-fed priest has sounded his ivory horn
by the altar, and we bear in platters heaped with steaming organ
   meats.
But if your livelihood depends on keeping herds and feeder
   calves,   195
or raising sheep and goats that browse a garden bare,
then seek the far-off woodland pastures of rich Taranto
and a plain like that unfortunate Mantua lost,
where a river full of water grasses feeds snow-white swans.
There your flocks will not lack flowing springs and ample
   grazing,   200
and however much your herds eat in the long, slow days,

that much the cold dew will replace in one short night.
Land that shows black and rich beneath the cutting plowshare,
land with a friable soil (imitated by our tilling)
is optimal for grain. From no other kind of field   205
will you see more wagons, pulled by slow oxen, heading home.
Or land where the plowman, all fired up, has clear-cut the woods,
leveling groves that have proved unfruitful through the years,
removing the deepest roots of the birds' immemorial
homes — forced from their nests, they seek the sky —   210
there the untilled plain shines beneath the driving plow.
But the dry gravel found in hill country scarcely
gives even humble senna and rosemary to the bees,
and the rough tufa and the chalk that black water snakes have
eaten out puts paid to the notion that any other lands   215
give food so sweet to snakes and so many holes to hide in.
But if the soil exhales shifting mists and transient vapors,
if it drinks in moisture that is released at will,
if it always clothes itself in fresh green grass and does not
damage the iron plow with darkening and salt-borne rust,   220
it will cover your elms with heavy-laden vines, will make
your olive trees fruitful and prove, as you cultivate it,
both nourishing for cattle and kind to your angled plow.
Capua tills such rich soil, like the volcanic stuff near Vesuvius
and the silt dumped on towns by Campania's flooding river.   225

    Now, I'll give guidelines on how to recognize each type.
If you want to know whether a soil is loamy or more
compact than usual (for one favors grain, the other wine;
dense belongs to Ceres, loam to the Body-Relaxer),
set your eye on a place and order a pit to be dug   230
deep in the earth, then put the dirt back in the hole
and level it by tamping it down with your feet.
If it no longer fills the hole, it is fertile loam

better suited to flocks and sweet vines, but if you can't replace
it all, and earth to spare spills out of the pit, then your field   235
has compact soil. Look for persistent clods and uneven
surfaces. Then break the obdurate ground with your strongest
    oxen.
But salty soil, the kind called sour (unfriendly
to crops, it is not improved by plowing, nor does it
preserve varietal grapes or the good name of fruit),   240
it will grant you this test: take down from the smoke-stained roof
your wicker baskets with close-woven splints and your wine
    strainers.
Adding sweet spring water, pack them to brimming over
with this worthless soil — and watch as every bit of water
runs out, flowing through the basket splints in juicy drops.   245
But taste will present undeniable evidence,
its sour nature puckering the testers' hapless mouths.
As for rich, friable soil, this is the way that we
recognize it: it hardly crumbles under kneading hands
but rather, like pitch, sticks to the fingers when it's held.   250
A moist soil is overexuberant, nourishing
a passel of weeds. Not for me, growth that's out of control —
may it not smother my grain stalks before they head.
A heavy soil mutely makes itself known by its weight;
so does a light one. The eye quickly spots a soil that's black   255
or any other color. But it's hard to discern
a cold that may kill; only pitch pine and poisonous yew
or black ivy sometimes show marks of its work.

    This understood, remember first to let your land bake
bone-dry in the sun, to cut deep trenches through the highest   260
ground and expose the plow-turned clods to the North Wind
before you plant the eager rootstocks of your vines. The best
    fields

have crumbly soil: the winds work it, and the cold hoarfrost,
along with the brawny spadesman who loosens acres as he moves.
But little escapes the notice of watchful men,   265
who look for just such soil—a plot with trees, first—to nurture
the vines, then the vineyard where they are transplanted so that
the young stock won't suddenly forget its distant mother.
No, farmers mark the quarters of heaven in the bark
and restore each new vine to its first orientation,   270
the front taking summer's heat, the back turned toward the north
    pole—
how powerful the innate habits of tender plants!
Think first on where to plant the vines—hillsides or flat land.
If you plot out rich fields on level ground, set them close;
that way, Bacchus does not hold back on their fruitfulness.   275
But if rolling terrain and gently sloping hills mark your land,
allow for elbowroom. When everything is put in place,
let squared-off paths cut neat right angles through the arbors.
As often in fierce war, when the legion deploys its companies
in long, straight ranks and the vanguard halts on an open plain,   280
the order of battle set, weapons glittering everywhere
moving like waves, and the troops bristle, spoiling to fight,
but War still wanders undecided between opposing sides—
just so, let your vineyard be governed by the same straight paths,
not simply because a pleasant view feeds an idle mind   285
but only so does earth give equal strength to all plants
and leave them open space to stretch out their branches.

    You may want to know how deep to dig your trenches.
I'd venture, yes, to set a vine in a shallow furrow
but secure the trees of the supporting arbor deep down,   290
especially the oak, for as high as its crown prods
breezy heaven, that deep do its roots probe hell.
This way, no winter storms, no gales nor hard-pelting rains

uproot it; it stays put, bound to endure, and outlasts many
generations, many human lifetimes as they roll on by.   295
Stretching out sturdy limbs and arms on all sides, standing
smack-dab in the center, it casts a huge green shade.

Don't set your vineyard on a slope facing the westering sun,
don't plant the hazel amid your vines, don't prune
the highest shoot or chop off cuttings from the treetops   300
(those close to earth are best), don't injure your seedlings
with a dull hatchet nor graft the trunk of a wild olive.
Be aware that undamped fire is often left behind
by thoughtless shepherds; hidden beneath the dry bark, it first
smolders in the wood and, stealing upward to the leaves,   305
roars skyward in a huge burst of flame; after that
rages, a victor, through branches and treetops
and rolls through all the grove out of control, erupting
skyward in a dense cloud of billowing, pitch-black darkness,
especially if foul weather from heaven broods over   310
the woods and a freshening wind fans the firestorm.
From fire, the strength in trunk and roots is lost, and trees cut
    down
do not come back nor rise from earth's depths to grow green
    again.
Only the useless wild olive with its bitter leaves survives.

Don't let some all-knowing busybody persuade you   315
to work unyielding soil when the wind blows out of the north.
Then, winter seizes farmland with black frost and does not let
a seedling's frozen roots fix themselves in the earth.
Vines are best planted when the white stork, rapacious
enemy of long snakes, arrives at the first flush of spring,   320
or else at summer's end before the first frosts of autumn,
when the speeding Sun's horses have not yet reached winter.

It is spring that decks the groves in leaves, spring that serves the
    woods;
in spring, Earth swells moistly and begs for bursting seed.
Then Sky, all-powerful father, descends to the womb   325
of his fertile spouse with inseminating rain and, uniting
his strength with her strong body, nourishes all they conceive.
The remotest thickets resound then with birdsong, and the herds
seek once again to mate in this appointed season.
The fair land longs to give birth; fields plowed but not yet sown
    open   330
themselves to the West Wind's ardor. Sweet moisture abounds
    for all.
Plants dare in safety to trust the sun's new light and warmth,
nor do the tendrils of the vines fear the South Wind's rising
or showers driven down from heaven by the forceful North Wind.
No, they sprout plump buds and unfurl all their leaves.   335
The same sunlight, no other, shone in the world's first days
and never, not once, changed its direction — in this
I trust. Spring was there, the whole world celebrated
spring, and the East Winds kept their wintry breath in check,
while the first cattle drank in the light, and earth's primal crop   340
of men lifted its head from the stony fields,
with game abounding in the woods, and stars, in the heavens.
Nor could delicate growth suffer seasonal extremes
without such respite between bitter cold and searing heat
and the continuation of heaven's tenderness toward earth.   345

    What's more, dress the cuttings that you set out in your
    garden
with rich manure and cover it, mind you, with plenty of soil,
or bury the cuttings in pumice or rough mussel shells,
for moisture will seep in, light breezes quietly arrive,
and the plants you've set lift up their spirits. Some, I've learned, 350

cover them with stones and large, heavy earthenware pots,
now as protection against hammering rains, later
when the scorching Dog Star bakes the land until it cracks.

Seedlings in place, it remains for you to cultivate
often around the roots and wield a vigorous hoe,   355
or work the soil under the plow's pressure and turn
your hardworking oxen down the rows of your vineyards.
Next, you prepare trellises — smooth reeds and props
stripped of bark, ash-wood stakes and sturdy forked branches.
    By these
the vines learn to climb and scoff at the winds, their canes   360
shooting up to the very crowns of the supporting elms.

But when they sprout new greenery in their early days,
leave the tender plants alone, and when the joyful vines thrust
skyward, speeding through cloudless air with loosened reins,
don't assault them with the sharp edge of your pruning hook,   365
but thin the leaves with fingers curved, gathering one here, one
    there.
Later, when they've reached the heights, their sturdy stems
    embracing
the elms, then clip off their foliage, then cut back their arms
(before they come to dread your knife), then, last of all,
exercise firm control and prune the rambunctious vines.   370

You must weave your hedge into a fence that excludes all
    cattle,
mainly when the leaves are young and know nothing of
    misfortune,
for over and above hard winters and searing sun,
wild bison, ever present, and pestiferous goats find sport
amid the vines; sheep graze there, and voracious heifers.   375

Not frigid weather bristling with silver hoarfrost
nor summer squatting heavy on parched and rocky hillsides
has wrought so much damage as the herds — the murder
in their hard teeth and the scar incised in the gnawed stem.
For no other offense, a goat is killed on every altar   380
for the Wine God, and old tragedies are brought to the stage.
Theseus' sons offer prizes for comedy in villages,
at crossroads, too; mid joyous carousing, they dance,
leaping and bounding on oiled goatskins laid on the soft fields.
Indeed, Italy's people, descended from Trojan stock,   385
make sport with rude verses and loud, unchecked belly laughs,
and they put on frightening masks made of curved bark.   .
It's *you*, Bacchus, whom they invoke with their rowdy songs,
for *you* the wooden heads they suspend to sway in the tall pines.
For this reason, every vineyard produces plump grapes,   390
the hollow valleys and deep woodland glades reach fullness,
and each place to which the god's handsome head has given the
      nod.
So, humbly, with our country's songs, we will sing the respect
due Bacchus and bring him heaping platters and holy cakes.
Then a billy goat, led by his horns, shall stand at the altar,   395
and the rich meat — we'll roast it on skewers of hazel.

      And you face yet other work in caring for your vines,
for which you can never do enough. Every year the soil
must be turned over three or four times, and the clods broken up
with your two-pronged hoe reversed, and the whole arbor   400
stripped of leaves. Moving in great circles, work revisits
the farmer as the year wheels around in its own tracks.
And as soon as the vineyard drops its leaves in the fall,
and the frigid North Wind shakes summer's beauty from the
      woods,
the passionate farmer extends his planning to the coming   405

year and attacks the dormant vine, cutting it back
with Saturn's curved pruning hook and trims it into shape.
Be the first to break up the earth, first to burn the cuttings
you've piled up, and first to store your support stakes in the shed.
Be the last to gather grapes. Twice, deep shade assaults your
    vines;   410
twice, weeds thick with thorny brambles overrun your vineyard.
Either task is hard work. Give praise to grand estates, but
farm one that's modest. Still more, prickly shoots of butcher's
    broom
throughout the woods and reeds on the riverbanks must be cut
    back;
dealing with wild willows will also keep you occupied.   415
Now the vines are bound, now leave off pruning the vineyard,
now the very last vine-dresser sings the completed rows.
You must still rake the soil, stirring up clouds of dust, and worry
that Jove may pummel your ripe grapes with hard rain.

    Olives are not like grapes. They require no tilling,   420
nor do they need pruning or the stiff-pronged rake.
Once they've rooted firmly and risen bold into the breezes,
Earth herself gives moisture and, opened by the curved plow,
yields as well a heavy crop of fruit. In this way
nurture the olive, rich and plump and cherished by Peace.   425

    And fruit trees, the moment they sense vigor in their trunks
and gain their full strength, shoot speedily heavenward
under their own power, hardly needing help from us.
Every grove, meanwhile, becomes no less laden with fruit,
and wilderness, beloved by birds, glows with flame-red berries.   430
Cattle graze on clover, the towering forest yields pine boards,
wood is tossed on nighttime fires, and they blaze up with light.
[How can men hesitate to sow and give their care?]

Why pursue a greater theme? Even willows and humble broom
offer leafage to the sheep or shade to the shepherd,   435
serviceable fencing, and nectar for honey.
Oh joy, to see boxwood on a windswept Anatolian
mountain and see Calabria's pine woods! Oh joy, to gaze on
fields ignorant of hoes and not beholden to man's care!
Even the infertile forests on Caucasian heights,   440
constantly buffeted and battered by the East Wind's blasts,
give us their products, some of one kind, some of another—
timber, pines for ships, cedars and cypresses to build our houses.
From these farmers fashion spokes for wheels or wooden
     cylinders
for their carts, and from these some men lay bent keels for boats.   445
Willows are fecund with withes, elms in foliage, but myrtle
and cornel cherry, brave in war, are lavish with iron-
hard spear shafts, and yews are bent into Syrian bows.
Nor do polished linden and boxwood, turned on a lathe,
fail to take shape, hollowed out by a sharp iron router.   450
Likewise, a craft of light alder wood, launched on the Po,
rides the ripping current, and swarming bees construct
their hives in hollowed cork trees or decaying hollies.
Have Bacchus' gifts brought us anything so remarkable?
Bacchus even offers cause for blame, as well: he made the
     Centaurs—   455
a stud, a son of Hell, a would-be rapist—so drunk
that they died when he threatened the Lapiths with his great jug.

     O farmers, abounding in good fortune, should they only
come to know their luck! For them, far from battle's din, the land
in its perfect fullness pours forth spontaneous nourishment.   460
What if a manor house with proud gates does not spew forth
a surge of those who've come to pay respects at dawn,
what if they never gape openmouthed at fine tortoiseshell

doorposts, clothes with gold thread, and Corinthian bronzes,
what if their snowy wool is not stained red with Assyrian dye   465
nor their olive oil adulterated with cinnamon —
they have untroubled sleep and lives unaware of deceit
but rich in overspilling plenty. The peace of broad acres,
caverns, lakes alive with fish, and cool valleys,
the lowing of cattle and tender dreams beneath the trees —   470
nothing is missing. They have woods, the retreat of game,
early years seasoned by work and sparse rations,
and reverence toward gods and forefathers. Among them, Justice,
abandoning the earth, made her final footprints.

But as for me, first may the Muses, sweet beyond all else,   475
whose sacred emblems I carry whelmed by a powerful
love, receive me and show me the journeys of stars through
   heaven,
the sun's eclipses, and the moon's ever-changing toil,
the reason for earth's tremors, the force that swells the high seas
till they break through their bounds, then lapse back into
   themselves,   480
and why suns in winter hurry to immerse themselves
in Ocean, or what delays make the cold nights so long.
But if the blood flows cold through my heart and so
bars me from entering nature's farthest reaches,
may rural land and streams rushing in its valleys please me.   485
May I, unrecognized, love its woods and waters! O those plains,
Thessalian rivers, and the mountains where Spartan girls hold
bacchanals! O that someone would put me in a steep-sided
Balkan valley and guard me with the shade of great branches!
Blessèd, he who understands the workings of nature   490
and tramples all fear and relentless fate and the bone-
shaking clatter of greedy Death beneath his feet.
And fortunate, he who knows the gods of the countryside —

Pan, Silvanus of the woods, and the sister Nymphs.
No public honor, no tyrants' purple has swayed him,   495
no discord driven him to break faith with his brothers.
He is not distressed by wild tribes, allied in war, that sweep down
from the Danube nor by Roman policies that destroy
kingdoms. He neither pities the poor nor envies the rich.
He gathers the fruits that his boughs, that his willing acres   500
readily yield and gives no thought to laws hard as iron,
the Forum's insanity, and the hall of public records.
Others slap their oars on dark, unknown seas, fall on their swords,
or thrust themselves into royal courts and palaces.
One man aims to destroy a city and its humble homes — just   505
to drink from a jeweled goblet and sleep on Tyrian purple;
another stores up treasures and broods on his buried gold.
Wide-eyed, one gawks at the Forum's speakers; another,
mouth agape, is swept away when lower class and upper both
applaud a statesman. Dripping with their brothers' gore,   510
they exult; exchanging familiar homes and hearths for exile,
they seek a fatherland that lies beneath a foreign sun.
The farmer has turned the soil over with his curved plow: in this,
the year's work; in this, sustenance for fatherland and small
grandchildren; in this, for herds of cows and worthy steers.   515
No time to relax, but the season abounds in fruits,
new calves and lambs, or sheaves of Ceres' grain, packing
the furrows with its growth and stuffing the granaries.
Winter comes: Peloponnesian olives are bruised in the press,
pigs come home plumped by mast, the woods yield red-berried
    arbutus;   520
autumn serves up its varied harvest, and terraced
on sun-warmed rocks, prime grapes reach their maturity.
Meanwhile, his sweet children linger around his kisses,
his pious home preserves its modesty, the bulging
udders of the cows let down much milk, and on the grass   525

the fat young goats, locking horns, butt at one another.
He himself takes a holiday. Relaxed on the grass
by a fire, his friends wreathing the jug, he invokes you,
First Wine-Maker, and pours a libation. For the herdsmen, he
    puts
targets on an elm for a javelin-hurling contest.   530
Some strip their muscled bodies bare for wrestling matches.
This is the kind of life the old Sabines cherished, as did
Remus and his brother. So Etruria grew strong,
and Rome truly became the world's most beautiful city,
enclosing her seven hills within a single wall.   535
Yes, before Jupiter picked up his scepter, before
an ungodly people gorged themselves on slaughtered steers,
golden Saturn lived this kind of life on earth.
No one had then heard the trumpet's blurted battle call
nor the sword's clatter when forged on an unyielding anvil.   540

    But now we've coursed in our race over a vast plain — it's time
to lift the harnesses from our horses' lathered necks.

BOOK THREE

You, we will sing, Goddess of Shepherds, and you, bright
　Apollo,
who fed Thessalian flocks, and you, Pan's sacred woods and streams.
Other poems, which may have beguiled idle minds with song,
　present
worn themes: who does not know of the king who set Hercules'
　labors
or the altars of the man-slaying king whom Hercules killed?　　　5
Who has not told of Hercules' lost friend, of Latona's Delos,
the bride Centaurs fought for, and Pelops the horse-tamer, marked
by an ivory shoulder? I must try for a new path on which I
may rise from the earth and soar triumphant from the lips of men.
First, returning to my homeland, if only I still breathe,　　　　10
I'll lead the Muses with me from the peak of Helicon.
First, I'll bring to you, Mantua my birthplace, palms from Judea
and build a temple of marble there on the green plain
near the water where the grand Mincio flows in lazy
bends and wears a fringe of slender rushes on his banks.　　　　15
I will place Caesar in the center, a god in his temple.
In his honor, I, the victor, striking in Tyrian purple,
will drive a hundred four-horse chariots beside the river.
For me, all Greece, quitting Olympia's stream and Nemea's groves,
shall vie in the races and with the weighted boxing glove.　　　　20

My head crowned with a wreath of trimmed olive leaves, I myself
will give the prizes. Even now it would please me to lead
the festive parade to your shrine, to see the steers sacrificed,
the stage scene changed as the sets revolve, and the red curtains
raised, so it seems, by the in-woven figures of Britons.   25
On the doors, in ivory and solid gold I will create
the East's warring tribes on the Ganges and the arms of victorious
    Romulus;
here, too, the Nile in flood, overflowing with battle,
and tall columns decked with the bronze beaks of our enemies'
    ships.
I will add Asia's conquered cities and Ararat struck down,   30
with the Parthians bold only in flight and volleys of arrows,
and the two trophies seized by might and main from distant foes,
the double triumph won on both Mediterranean shores.
Statues of Parian marble shall stand there breathing — Aeneas'
forebears and descendants, the names of the nation sent down   35
by Jove, and the namesake of Troy, and Apollo, Troy's builder.
Hapless Envy shall quake before the Furies and Hell's wailing
river, before Ixion's manacles of twisted snakes
and his monstrous wheel, before the stone that always rolls back
    down.
Meanwhile, Maecenas, let us seek to attain the Dryads' woods   40
and untried glades, in accord with your not so easy command.
Without you my mind attempts no serious thought. Go then,
    break
with sluggish delay. The Muses' mountain sounds a ringing
    summons,
as do the Spartan hunting hounds, and Epidaurus, mistress
of horses, and the call, doubled by applauding groves, rings back.   45
Yet soon I will arm myself to tell of Caesar's fiery
battles and assure his name's praise through as many years
as Caesar is distant from the birth of Dawn's consort.

Whether a man, yearning for a prize of Olympian palms,
rears horses, whether he raises oxen strong at the plow,   50
he must look chiefly at maternal conformation. The best
cow has a wild-eyed look, her head ugly, her neck massive,
with dewlaps that hang from her jaw as far down as her knees;
then, there's no limit to her long flank — everything's large,
even her hooves and the shaggy ears below her crooked horns.   55
Nor would a cow distinguished by white spots displease me,
one refusing the yoke and sometimes ready with her horns,
resembling a bull in appearance, of great height
with her tail brushing the imprints of her hooves as she walks.
The age for calving and proper insemination   60
ends before the tenth year and begins after the fourth;
in other years, she's not fit for breeding nor strong with the plow.
Meanwhile, as long as fertile youth prevails in the herds,
let the males loose; take the lead in sending livestock to mate
and, by breeding them, supply generations of calves.   65
The best day of a lifetime is the first to flee for luckless
humankind; sickness comes in stealth, with graceless old age
and suffering, and death's relentless rigor seizes us.
There shall always be cows whose shape you'd like to change;
yes, always rebuild and, lest you later question your losses,   70
plan for the future and yearly choose new stock for the herd.

For your herd of horses there is likewise no other choice.
But to those you'd rear for stud in hope for the species,
devote special care to them from the time they are foals.
From the first, a colt of the best lineage walks in the fields   75
with a higher step and brings his feet down lightly.
He dares to go first on the path, to test raging rivers
and commit himself to unfamiliar bridges,
nor does he bolt at untoward sounds. His neck is arched,

his head graceful, his belly trim and back plumped out,   80
and his proud chest abounds in muscle. The finest
colors are chestnut and gray, the worst white and dun.
Then, if he hears the faraway sound of clashing arms,
he cannot stand still, his ears prick forward, his limbs quiver,
and, whickering, he snorts the gathered fires from his nostrils.   85
His mane is lush and, tossed, falls back on his right shoulder;
his backbone's double ridge runs along his loins, and his hoof
hollows earth, thundering loudly on its wall of horn.
Such was the stallion Cyllarus, broken in by Pollux
of Sparta; those, too, that Greek poets remember —   90
Mars' two horses yoked abreast and the team of great Achilles.
So, too, was Saturn himself when he became a horse on his wife's
arrival and raced away, fugitive, tossing his mane
over his neck and filling Pelion's heights with his whinny.

Put even this horse in his stall when he weakens, burdened   95
by illness or slowed by his years; don't pity his sorry
old age. An aged stud is cold to sex and takes on the thankless
task to no avail, and when he ventures into battle,
his rage is empty as a flash fire burning without strength
through dry stalks. Therefore make special note of spirit and age,   100
then of other qualities, other offspring of the sires and dams,
and the sorrow each shows in defeat, the pride in victory.
You see, don't you, when chariots take to the field in headlong
competition and rush forth, poured out of the starting gate,
when hope excites young drivers, that care, run riot, drains   105
their pounding hearts? They press on, whips flailing, and leaning
forward slacken the reins. Filled with force, the heated wheels
    roll on.
Now low to the ground, now lifted aloft, the horses seem
to be borne through the empty air and ascend into heaven.

No pausing, no rest, but a cloud of yellow dust rises,   110
they're lathered with foam and the snorting of those hot on their
    heels—
so fierce their love of praise, so strong their desire for victory.
Vulcan's regal son first dared harness a team of four
to the chariot and stood, a victor, over the racing wheels.
Thessalians on horseback in Centaur country gave bridle   115
and training ring to us and taught a rider in full armor
to gallop over the field, then bring those proud steps to a trot.
For war or the races, the task is equal, and, equally,
trainers judge a young horse by ardent spirit and zeal to run,
though another horse may often have routed the enemy,   120
have called Epirus or powerful Mycenae his homeland,
and claimed descent from the horse that Neptune struck into
    being.

    These things noted, the trainers move on at the right time for
        mating
and devote all care to fill out with solid flesh the horse
that is chosen as leader and named as stud for the herd.   125
For him, cut clover in flower and supply fresh water
and grain so he will not fail to excel at his lusty
work nor sire puny foals because his feed runs short.
But stockmen keep the herd of broodmares lean on purpose,
and when the pleasure that they'll come to know first rouses
    mares   130
to mate, stockmen deny leafy fodder and bar them from springs.
Often, too, they make the mares gallop and tire them in the sun
at the time that the floor groans as grain is threshed with repeated
blows and when the empty chaff is cast to the rising West Wind.
They do this to assure that excess does not dull the unsown,   135
generative soil nor fill its idle furrows with mud;
then it may thirstily grasp the seed and suck it in deep.

Then, care for the sires begins to fall off and that for the dams
to ascend. When their months are accomplished and they wander
    great
with young, no one should let them strain against the yokes of
    heavy   140
wagons, go leaping ahead, graze the meadows in skittish
fits and starts, or swim in the rip currents of a river.
They pasture in the open woods beside streams full
of water, where moss and the greenest grass grow on the banks,
with caves as shelter, and the long shadow of high rocks.   145
A swarming fly infests the groves by the river Sele
and the evergreen oaks of Lucanian mountains. Its Roman
name is gadfly, while the Greeks, making a change, call it *oestrus*.
Cruel, with a shrill whine, it causes whole herds, terrified,
to run through the woods. Shattered by their bawling, air rages,   150
and so do the woods and the banks of the dry Black River.
Once Juno used this monster to vent her terrible wrath,
bringing the pest into being for the heifer Io.
Keep it away from the gravid cows, because it bites
more viciously in noonday heat, pasture the herds   155
just after sunrise or when the stars lead in the night.

    After birth all diligence is transferred to the calves;
then the farmers brand them with the mark and name of their
    breed
and set aside those to rear to perpetuate their kind,
to keep as sacred for the altar, or to cultivate earth   160
and turn over the uneven field breaking its clods.
The rest of the cattle pasture on green grasses, but train
those that you'll prepare for work and service on the farm
when they are still calves and set them on the path to dociling
while their youthful spirits are willing, while their lives are
    tractable.   165

First of all, tie loose circles of slender withes around
their shoulders; then, when once-free necks become accustomed
to such servitude, yoke the oxen in pairs, joined
at the collars, and make them step together.
Let them also pull empty carts over the ground   170
and stamp the prints of their hooves on its dusty surface.
Later, let the hardworking beechwood axle creak under
a mighty load and a bronze-covered pole pull the joined wheels.
Meanwhile, do not fodder your unbroken steers only
on grass or willow leaves and sedge from the swamp but also   175
add kernels of grain picked by hand, nor will your most fecund
cows fill the snowy pails in the fashion of our fathers
but rather let down their udders' milk to their sweet calves.

     But if you've more passion for war and bold squadrons of
     horse
or gliding on wheels past Pisa's Olympian waters   180
and driving a winged chariot in Jupiter's wild olive grove,
the horse's first task is to stand steady when arms confront him,
endure the cavalry's shrill trumpet, put up with creaking
wheels as they roll, and hear the bridles clink in the tack room;
then, more and more, to find pleasure in the caress of his   185
trainer's praise and to love the sound of his neck being stroked.
And let him know this as soon as he's weaned from his mother's
teat; let him gradually venture giving his mouth to soft halters
while still unready and trembling, still ignorant of life.
But after three summers, when the fourth draws near, let him   190
soon begin to use the training ring, to make his steps sound
rhythmically, to flex his legs in alternating curves,
to be like a true worker. Then let him summon the wind
to a race and, flying over an open expanse as if
free from the reins, let him barely touch the sand with his hooves,   195
as when a continuing North Wind bears down from its

fabled source in the Arctic, spreading far and wide Asia's storms
and dry clouds; then the tall wheat and the rain-soaked plains
   tremble
under light breezes, the highest leaves in the forest
rustle, and long combers roll in toward the shore;   200
wind soars, cleansing the fields and the waters at once in his flight.
A horse like this will sweat, shaking bloody foam from his mouth
toward the Olympian markers and over the plains' racecourse, or
   he'll
better draw with his obedient neck a Gallic war chariot.
Then, at last, when he is broken, let his body grow   205
to a noble size on ample mixed grain; but before breaking,
his spirit will flare high and hot and, caught, he'll refuse to mind
a snapping whip or suffer a curb made harsh with spikes.

   But no other effort strengthens vigor more than keeping
the scent of heat at bay and the blind pricks of love,   210
whether you prefer to work with cattle or with horses.
So, stockmen send a bull far away to isolated
pastures, beyond a mountain range and across broad rivers,
or keep him penned inside with feed trough as full as possible.
Just seeing a female little by little tears at his strength   215
and consumes him, nor do her seductive charms allow him
to remember the groves and grassy meadows. She incites
her proud lovers to fight for victory with their long horns.
A shapely heifer grazes in the pinewoods of the south:
by turns, inflicting deep wounds, the bulls tangle in battle   220
with great force, blood so dark that its black drips from their
   bodies,
and amid deafening bellows, tossed horns are driven home
in both contenders; earth and heaven reverberate with echoes.
Foes do not share the same stable and herd; rather, the loser
departs to live in far-off exile in an unknown land   225

bawling loudly about his disgrace and the blows struck
by the proud winner, about love lost and never avenged,
and, looking sadly at his stable, leaves the kingdom of his line.
So he works on his strength with tireless care and lies nightlong
amid hard rocks in a covered den, while feeding by day   230
on prickly leaves and sharp blades of sedge. And he tests himself—
tackling a tree trunk, he learns to gather his rage
in his horns; with repeated stabs he assaults the wind
and practices for combat on sand scattered by his hooves.
With energy collected and strength restored, he takes up   235
the standards and races headlong at his oblivious foe,
as when a wave begins to curl, foaming white, out at sea,
it rises ever longer from the deeps and, rolling ashore
tall as a mountain, crashes wildly on the rocks
and collapses, but underneath, the water boils up   240
in whirlpools and flings black sand high in the air.

        Every last species on earth, man and beast alike,
the vast schools of the sea, the cattle and bright-colored birds
fall helpless into passion's fire: love is the same for all.
At no other time does the lioness, forgetting her cubs,   245
roam the grasslands more fiercely, or the hulking bear
deal more death and ruin everywhere throughout the forests;
then the boar is savage, then the tiger, most destructive;
oh, then it is not safe to wander Libya's lonely fields.
You see, don't you, that quivering pervades every last bit   250
of horseflesh when the scent is wafted on an intimate breeze?
Not the riders' reins nor a lashing whip hold them back,
not crags and overhanging cliffs nor surging rivers
that have eroded mountains and flung them to the waves.
As for the Sabine boar, he runs flat out and sharpens his tusks,   255
scrapes up the earth with his hoof, rubs his flanks on the trees,
and hardens his shoulders on this side and that against wounds.

What of young Leander in whose bones love unrelenting
lights its huge fire? In the fury of whirling windstorms
late in the dark night, he swims the straits. Above him heaven's   260
vast portal thunders, and waves breaking on the cliffs echo
the booming. His worried parents cannot call him back,
or the beloved girl who will die on his battered corpse.
What of Bacchus' mottled lynxes and the lusty species
of wolves and dogs? What of the fights that rut brings to peaceful
    stags?   265
The notable passion of mares, of course, exceeds all others;
Venus herself gave this instinct when an unbred team
of four, using teeth to rip off his limbs, killed their master.
Love leads them over Mount Ida and over the wide stream that
roars to the Black Sea; they climb mountains and swim across
    rivers.   270
The moment the flame is lit in their yearning marrow
(mostly in spring, for in spring the fever returns to their bones),
nostrils turned to the West Wind, they all stand on high cliffs
and sniff the light breezes. Then, often without any
coupling, pregnant by the wind (oh, strange to relate),   275
they scatter over rocks and crags and low-lying valleys
not toward your rising, East Wind, nor that of the Sun,
but to the North and Northeast Winds or else where the blackest
South Wind begins to blow, darkening heaven with freezing rain.
At last, the viscous "mare-madness," as herdsmen rightly name it,   280
oozes slowly from the vulva — mare-madness, the creamy
mucus that wicked stepmothers often collect to mix
with herbs and spoken spells that are far from harmless.

But meanwhile time flies, it flies beyond recovery
while, captive to each fact, we are carried away by love.   285
Enough about herds! The other part of my interests asserts
itself — to tend the woolly flocks and shaggy nanny goats.

This is hard work; hence steadfast countrymen hope for acclaim.
Nor does my heart doubt how glorious it is to conquer
these matters with words and give their humbleness grace.   290
But sweet love propels me over Mount Parnassus' lonely
heights; it brings joy to traverse the summits where no earlier
path leads down an easy slope to the Muses' fountain.
Now, holy Shepherdess, now we must sing you with full voice.

   To begin with, I ordain that sheep be fed on grass   295
in soft enclosures till summer soon brings back its leaves,
and that you spread out straw and handfuls of fern
over the hard ground so that frigid ice does not damage
young sheep—giving them foul foot-rot and wool lumpy with
   scab.
Proceeding onward, I exhort you to supply your goats   300
with arbutus leaves and provide access to a fresh stream
and place their pens away from the wind, facing the south
and the winter sun at the time that Aquarius begins
to set and sprinkle the end of the year with cold rain.
The nannies, too, must be tended with no trifling care, and profit   305
from their milk will be no less, although Anatolian wool
dyed in Tyrian purple is traded for a high price.
From them, sturdier kids; from them, a great plenty of milk;
the more the pail brims with foam from the emptying udder,
the more free the rivers that stream from pressure on the teats.   310
Not less, meanwhile, do herdsmen cut the beards from the hoary
chins of Libyan billy goats and shear their coarse hair
to use in soldiers' tents and jackets for shivering seamen.
They browse in the woods, yes, and on Arcadian summits,
feeding on sharp brambles and thorny shrubs that love steep
   places;   315
leading their kids, they themselves remember to come home,

and they barely clear the doorstep with their bulging udders.
Thus, the less their want for human care, the more eagerly
you should protect them from ice and snow-bearing winds,
cheerfully providing them with hay and brushy fodder,   320
nor should you ever close your hayloft for the whole winter.

But, when joyful summer at the West Wind's bidding sends
both sheep and goats into the woods, into the pastures,
let us go to the chilly fields as the Morning Star
rises, while the day is new, while the grass still glistens   325
and the dew on its green blades most appeals to the cattle.
Then, when the fourth hour of heaven builds dryness and thirst
and the arbors erupt with the song of complaining cicadas,
I shall bid the flocks beside wells and deep standing pools
to drink the water that burbles down into oaken troughs.   330
But in midday swelter, let them seek out a shady hollow
wherever Jupiter's oak with its strong old trunk
stretches out its enormous branches or wherever
a grove, dark with holm oaks, lies in numinous shadow.
Then give them trickling water again and feed them again   335
till sundown when the cool Evening Star tempers the air,
the moon, filled with dew, renews the woodland pastures, and
     shores
resound with the kingfisher, stands of thistle with the goldfinch.

Why tell you in verse of Libyan shepherds, why tell of their
pastures and the encampments where they live in scattered huts?   340
Often, day and night, for a whole month at a time,
the flock grazes and wanders the vast desert without any
sheepfolds — the plain stretches to the horizon. The African
herdsman takes everything with him — hut and household gods
and weapons and his best dog and his finest quiver.   345

Just so, the zealous Roman, bearing his country's arms,
marches on at full speed despite a heavy load and, sooner
than the enemy expects, halts his troops to pitch camp.

　　Not so with the Scythian people by the Sea of Azov,
where the turbid Danube tosses its bleached sands　　　　　　350
and the Thracian range stretched toward the North Pole turns
　　South again.
They keep their flocks penned in sheepfolds and do not provide
them with grass from the plain nor leaves from the trees, for the
　　land
lies shapeless everywhere under drifts of snow and thick
layers of ice that pile up more than a dozen feet deep.　　　　355
It's always winter, always Northwest Winds blowing cold.
There the Sun scarcely ever disperses the pale shadows,
not when, drawn by his horse, he seeks high heaven, nor when
he bathes his fast-diving chariot in Ocean's red plain.
Sudden crusts of ice increase on a flowing current,　　　　　360
and the water sustains iron-covered wheels on a surface
hospitable once to ships but now to wide wagons.
Bronze commonly breaks apart, and the clothes on their backs
stiffen and freeze, and they use axes to chop up once-liquid
wine, and lakes clear to the bottom turn into solid ice,　　　365
and the pointed icicle hardens on a shaggy beard.
Meanwhile, no less than cold, snow everywhere fills the sky.
The cattle die, the oxen's massive bodies stand enclosed
in drifts, and the deer, crowded into compact herds, are numbed
by the strange weight, with just the tips of their horns to be seen.　370
These they do not hunt with dogs released or strung-out nets
or the scarlet feather meant to scare them into running,
but, iron blade in hand, they strike the deer, trying in vain
to breast the mountain of snow, and kill them as they bleat

loudly and carry them off with a fierce cry of joy.   375
They themselves lead leisurely, carefree lives in caves dug
deep under the earth where they roll piles of oak logs
and even whole elm trees into the hearth to feed the fire.
Here they spend the night in play and happily imitate
the vineyard's drinks by fermenting sour serviceberry juice.   380
Such is the unchecked breed of men lying beneath the Great Bear's
seven stars in the far north, blasted by the cold East Wind,
and covering their bodies with the tawny hides of wild beasts.

If wool is your goal, first remove damaging stands
of burs and star thistles, avoid pastures with high grass,   385
and without delay select white flocks with soft fleeces.
But if a ram, no matter that his pelt gleams white, shows
a black tongue beneath the moist roof of his mouth,
scorn him lest he sully the wool of newborn lambs
with spots, and look for another in your abounding flock.   390
With a gift of such snow white wool, if we can believe it,
Pan, the god of Arcadia, caught and deceived you, Moon,
calling you into the deep woods, nor did you spurn his call.

But for him who loves milk, let his own hand bring abundant
clover and other trefoils to the goat pens, and salted hay.   395
From this, the more they crave fresh water, the more their udders
swell, and their milk bears a light hint of saltiness.
Many also separate the kids from their mothers
and from their first day close their mouths with iron-covered
     muzzles.
From the milking at dawn or during daylit hours, they press   400
cheese at night; by day, from the milking after dark or
at sunset. They send it out in wicker baskets — a herdsman
takes it to town — or salt it lightly to store for the winter.

   Don't let dogs be the last of your concerns, but feed your
   swift
Spartan pups and spirited Molossian hounds alike   405
on fattening whey. Never, while they keep watch, need you
fear a nocturnal thief in your pens and a raid
by wolves or unpacified brigands behind your back.
Often, too, you'll give chase to the wild ass
and with dogs hunt down the hare, with dogs the fallow deer.   410
Often you'll disturb a boar in his forest wallows,
routing him with dogs giving tongue, or with clamorous baying
you'll pursue a stag over the high rocks into a net.

   Learn, as well, to burn fragrant cedar in your folds and drive
   out
the foul-smelling water snake with fumes of resinous sap.   415
Often underneath neglected pens a viper, deadly
to the touch, lies hidden and fearfully avoids the daylight,
or an adder, usually found sheltering right under a roof,
descends, a harsh plague to cattle, and hugs earth to bespatter
the herd with its venom. Grab stones, herdsman, grab a strong
   branch,   420
and as it rises in menace, neck swollen with hissing,
strike it down. Now in retreat, it hangs its frightened head low
while its central coil and the motion of its slithering tail
are loosened, and the last curve slowly drags its sinuous course.
There's also that deadly amphibious snake found   425
in Calabria's groves, coiling its scaly back with breast
raised high and its long belly marked with distinctive spots.
While any streams burst fluent from their sources and while
the earth is moist with spring showers and the rainy South Winds,
he abides by pools, living on the banks where, insatiable,   430
he crams his deadly black gullet with fish and croaking frogs.

After the marsh has burned up and summer drought cracks the
    earth,
he races to dry land and, darting his fiery eyes,
desperate with thirst, maddened by heat, vents his fury in the
    fields.
Let it not please me then to catch up with sleep under the open   435
sky nor sprawl on my back in the grass of a wooded glade
when, his old skin sloughed, fresh and sleek with youth, he
loops and twists onward, his young or eggs left behind,
and rising sunward, he flickers from his maw a three-forked
    tongue.

Disease, as well, its causes and symptoms, I will teach you.   440
Crusty scab attacks sheep when freezing rain and winter,
bristling with hoarfrost, settle deep in their quick,
or when high summer's dirty sweat has clung to the shorn
flock and prickly brambles have cut through their skin.
Therefore the herdsmen dip the whole flock in fresh water,   445
and the ram is immersed in the stream till his fleece is
sodden and he is released to float down on the current.
Or, after shearing, they apply harsh olive oil lees
to the body mixing in silver slag and natural
sulphur, pitch from Mount Ida, wax rich in oil,   450
squill, as well, and strong hellebore and black bitumen.
Yet no other work on a sheep's behalf is more powerful than
being able to open the deep source of an abscess
with a knife: the harm is nourished and lives by concealment
when the shepherd refuses to lay healing hands on the sore   455
and just sits there imploring the gods for better omens.
What's more, when spreading pain rages deep in the bones
of the bleaters and a parching fever feeds on their joints,
it is useful to avert hot inflammation and deep

down in the hoof to lance a vein, pulsing with blood,   460
as is the custom of Macedonians and the shrewd Scythian
when he migrates to the Thracian mountains, and the wild tribes
along the Danube who drink milk thickened with horses' blood.
If you should see a sheep often head far away
into soft shade, or nibble listlessly at the tops of grass   465
while lagging behind, or fall in the middle of the field
as it grazes and go off alone late at night, check
the problem immediately with the knife before the dire
infection spreads contagion through the whole heedless flock.
A spinning whirlwind does not rush off the sea so thick with
   storms   470
as does a host of plagues for the group, nor do they snatch away
a single animal but a whole summer sheepfold at once—
the flock and its offspring and the whole species, both old and
   young.
Then anyone would understand were he to witness now
what happened long before—lofty Alps, Danube hill forts, river-   475
watered fields on Adriatic shores, the abandoned kingdoms
of shepherds, their woodland pastures empty far and wide.

    Here, at one time, from an afflicted sky a season
to lament broke out and glowed with the full heat of autumn.
It brought death to all domestic animals, all wild beasts,   480
and it tainted their water, poisoned their fodder with sickness.
Nor did the sickness take a straight path, but when fiery thirst
driven through every vein had contracted their limbs,
then a watery fluid spilled over and bit by bit
dissolved into itself all the bones ruined by disease.   485
Often, mid holy rites, a victim standing by the altar
while a woolen band with a snowy garland was fastened on
its head, has collapsed, dying in front of the unprepared priests.
Or, before that, if the celebrant makes sacrifice with the knife,

then high altars do not come alight with entrails laid thereon,   490
nor can the seer give a response when he's consulted,
and the sacrificial knife is barely tinged with blood,
and only the sand's top layer is darkened by scant serum.
From this cause, calves everywhere die in the lushest grass
or surrender their sweet lives beside full feeding troughs;   495
from this cause, rabid madness comes to friendly dogs, and a
    gasping
cough makes sick pigs tremble and chokes them with swollen
    throats.
The stricken horse, once a victor, stumbles, forgetting both
zest and grass; he turns away from water and often strikes
the ground with a hoof; his ears droop, on them a fitful sweat   500
breaks out, turning cold when he is about to die; his skin
is dry and, unyielding to the touch, resists his handler.
In the first days these are the signs of approaching death,
but as the sickness progresses, it begins to rage.
Then, truly, the eyes burn, and breath is drawn deeply inward,   505
heavy now and then with groans, and the nethermost flanks
are distended by drawn-out gasping, from the nostrils
black blood pours, and the rough tongue presses on the blocked
    throat.
It seemed helpful to infuse them with wine through an inserted
funnel — this was thought the one salvation for the dying,   510
but soon it led to their failing — they burned up with madness
renewed, and already sick unto death (may the gods grant
better to the pious and injury like that to our foes),
they tore at their limbs, cutting them to pieces with bared teeth.
But look, the ox, smoking under the heavy plowshare,   515
collapses and vomits blood mixed with foam from his mouth
and groans in his extremity. The sorrowing
plowman goes, unyoking the ox that mourns its brother's death,
and in the midst of the job leaves the plow idle.

Not the shade of the deep groves, not the soft grassy meadows   520
can stir his spirit, not the stream clearer than amber rolling
down rocks as it seeks the plain; his flanks sag loose
beneath him, and dullness afflicts his sluggish gaze,
and his neck, under a pressing weight, hangs down toward the
    earth.
What use his work and services? What use that he turned   525
hard earth with the plow? Yet neither Bacchus' gifts from wine-rich
Campania nor recurrent banquets harmed him and his kind.
They feed on leaves and fodder of plain grass, their cups are
upwelling springs and rivers flowing rapid in their
course, nor does care disrupt the sleep that brings them health.   530
At that time and no other, so they say, in those regions
cattle were sought in vain for Juno's rites and chariots
were drawn by mismatched wild oxen to her high temple.
So men feebly hack at the soil with hoes and bury
seeds with their own fingernails and, straining their necks,   535
drag creaking wagons over the high hills.
The wolf does not attempt an ambush beside the sheepfold
nor stalk the flocks by night; a more consuming care
domesticates him. Shy fallow deer and stags quick to bolt
now come and go among the dogs and around the houses.   540
Back then, the wide sea's progeny, yes, the whole tribe of
    swimmers —
the waves washed them up at shore's edge like shipwrecked
    corpses;
in unusual fashion, seals fled upriver.
The viper, too, guarded in vain by its crooked retreats,
expires, as do the water snakes, their scales erect.   545
The air is not kind, even to birds, and they,
plummeting headlong, leave life beneath the high clouds.
Moreover, it does not help to change the diet now,
and the medicines given work harm; the experts fail —

the centaur Chiron and Melampus, the world's first physician.   550
Sent from Stygian darkness into the light, the pallid Fury
Tisiphone rages, driving before her Fever and Fear,
and, growing day by day, lifts ever higher her ravenous head.
Rivers and their parched banks and the sloping hills resound
with the bleating of flocks and the herds' recurrent bawling.   555
And now, wholesale, she wreaks carnage and piles up rotted
bodies, foul and stinking, in the barns themselves — till people
learn to cover them with earth and bury them in pits.
For, the hides were of no use, and the sickness in the flesh
could not be destroyed by water nor overcome by fire.   560
Men could not shear off the wool, eaten up as it was
by sickness and filth, nor touch the spun threads.
Truly, if anyone touched that detestable clothing,
inflamed pustules and dirty sweat would break out all down
his foul arms and legs, nor did he wait a long time   565
before the unholy fire ate his infected limbs.

BOOK FOUR

The sky's celestial gift of honey — now I'll follow up
with that. Maecenas, look with approval on this part as well.
The wonder-stirring drama of a tiny state,
its great-hearted leaders and the entire species' habits
and pursuits and swarms and battles — of these I shall tell you.   5
Trivial the work, but hardly trivial the glory if
unlucky powers so permit and Apollo heeds one's prayers.

    First, you must seek a fixed abode for the bees, to which
the winds may find no entry because the winds prevent them
from bearing home their food; in which no sheep and head-
      butting goats   10
may cavort amid the flowers, no wandering heifer shake
the dew from the pasture and injure the growing grass.
And let bright-colored lizards with scaly backs be absent
from the rich stables, along with the bee-eater and other
birds, like the swallow, Procne, breast stained by her bloody hands,   15
for all, far and wide, will be ruined as birds, catching bees
on the wing, bring them by bill as sweet tidbits for fierce nestlings.
But let springs welling clear and pools green with moss
be present, and a tiny rivulet hurrying through the grass,
and let a palm or giant wild olive shade the entrance   20
so that, when the new kings lead forth the first swarms in spring,

which is their time, and released from the comb, the young bees
    frolic,
a nearby stream bank may invite them to retire from the heat
and a tree in their path hold them within its welcoming leaves.
In the midst of the water, be it still or free-flowing,   25
place willows across it or stones that look huge to the bees,
so that they can alight on bridges placed close together
and spread their wings to the summer sun if a sudden East Wind
has sprinkled those that dally or plunged them into Neptune's
    realm.
Let green and fragrant laurel flower all around — wild thyme,
    as well,   30
broadcasting its perfume, and much strong-smelling savory,
and let banks of violets drink at a thirst-quenching spring.
As for your beehives, be they made of hollow bark sewn
together or woven from a willow's pliant twigs,
let them have narrow entrances, for with its cold, winter   35
thickens the honey, while heat thins it to a liquid.
Either force must be feared equally by the bees, and not
in vain do they vie to daub wax in the tiny holes
of their houses, plaster the openings with waxy cement
made from flower buds, and, for this purpose, keep stores of glue   40
more adhesive than birdlime or pitch from Mount Ida.
Often, if rumor is true, they also make a snug home
in secret places dug out underground; they're found as well
deep in pumice stone's holes and the hollows of decaying trees.
For all that, to keep them cozy, smear smooth mud in the cracks   45
of their chambers and throw a few leaves on the outside.
Do not let yew grow close to the hive nor cook reddening
crabs at your hearth nor put credence in deep marshes
or a place where the smell of muck is strong or where hollow
    rocks
ring when stuck, and that voice reverberates, echo on echo.   50

For the rest, when golden Sun has driven winter
into exile beneath the earth and opened the sky with summer
light, at once they roam everywhere through glades and groves,
rifling the bright flowers and sipping lightly on the surface
of the streams. Hence, by some sweet joy that I cannot know,   55
they cherish their progeny and nests; therefore, with skill
they mold fresh wax and fashion their sticky honey.
Therefore, when you look up and see the swarm, newly released,
mounting through clear summer air and the starry heavens,
and you marvel at the dark cloud streaming in the wind,   60
take close note: always they seek out sweet waters and leafy
bowers. Here you are to scatter traditional dainties —
rubbed bee balm and honeywort's plant, commonly found; raise
a clangor, too, shaking the Great Mother's cymbals all around.
They themselves will settle in fragrant abodes, they themselves,   65
after their fashion, will hide in the innermost cradles.

But if they have flown forth to battle — for often discord
accompanied by great agitation befalls two kings,
right then, from a distance, you may discern the mob's
temper and the feelings stirred by war, for that martial call   70
from hoarse-resonating brass blares to those that dally,
and a tone like the broken blurting of trumpets is heard;
then, restless, they come together, their wings vibrate and flash,
they sharpen their stings with their mouthparts and ready their
    strength;
around the king and to his royal tent itself, they swarm   75
densely, summoning the enemy with a great clamor;
therefore, when they've gained a bright spring day and an open
    field,
they burst from the gates to join battle, high in the air
the sound buzzes, mingled they're gathered into a great ball
and suddenly plummet — no denser is hail from the air   80

nor so heavy acorns raining from a shaken oak.
Among the armies, the kings themselves, with enormous wings,
keep their large souls pulsing in very small breasts,
resolute always not to retreat until a strong victor
has forced one side or the other to turn its back in flight.   85
This tumult of passion and these overwhelming struggles
are brought to rest, checked, by the tossing of a little dust.

But when you've called both generals back from the
    battleground,
kill him that looks more sorry lest he cause waste and harm;
let the better rule alone in the empty inner court.   90
The one shall blaze with rough spots of gold,
for there are two kinds of kings: the better is both handsome
in countenance and bright with red spots; the other, uncouth
with idleness and shamefully dragging his drooping belly.
As the kings' forms are two, so the bodies of the commoners.   95
For, some look rough and ugly, as when a parched traveler
emerges from deep dust and spits on the ground from a dry
    mouth;
the others shine and flash with the brilliance of lightning,
their bodies ablaze and adorned with uniform golden speckles.
They are the more capable species; from them in time's fullness,   100
you'll extract sweet honey, though not so much sweet as clear
and able to overcome the acidic flavor of wine.

But when the swarms fly without purpose and make sport
    aloft,
disdaining their honeycombs and leaving their houses cold,
keep these erratic spirits from engaging in useless play.   105
It's not much work to keep the bees down: rip off the royal
wings; while the kings stay put, not one bee will dare
to take flight upward or pull the banners from the camp.

Let gardens fragrant with golden flowers invite them,
and let him who watches for thieves and birds, Priapus,   110
the Hellespont's guardian, protect them with his willow pruning
   hook.
May he himself to whom such care accrues set thyme and sweet
viburnum brought from the high hills all around their homes;
himself toughen his hands with hard work, setting out
plants in the earth and watering them with friendly moisture.   115

     And truly, with my work now near its end, were I not
lowering my sails and hastening to turn the prow toward land,
perhaps I should also sing what careful cultivation
adorns rich gardens and the rose beds of twice-bearing Paestum,
and how endives rejoice in the streams that they drink   120
and the green banks, in celery, and how the cucumber
sprawling through the grass swells into a paunch. Nor should I be
silent about late-blooming narcissus or the flexible
twigs of acanthus, pale ivy, and shore-loving myrtle.
For, I recall that under Spartan-founded Taranto's   125
fortress-towers, where the black Galeno waters golden wheat fields,
I saw an old man from Asia Minor who had a few
rural acres, not fertile enough to be plowed by oxen
nor suitable for the flock's grazing nor fit for the vine.
Nonetheless, here amid brambles, planting vegetables in rows,   130
white lilies, curative vervain, and slender-stemmed poppies,
he equaled the wealth of kings in spirit and, coming home
late at night, loaded his tables with an unbought feast.
He was the first to pick roses in spring and apples in fall,
and when harsh winter still broke apart the rocks   135
with its cold and curbed the flow of water with ice,
he was cutting away the asphodel's limp foliage,
rebuking tardy summer and the dallying West Winds.
So, he was first to be rich in productive bees

and a bountiful swarm, first to collect foaming honey pressed   140
from the comb, and his lime trees and pines were most luxuriant;
as many the fruits in new flower that clothed his fertile trees,
so many did they hold into autumn's fullness.
He also, though the season was late, set elms out in rows
and pears hardened to weather and grafted blackthorns bearing   145
plums as well as plane trees providing drinkers with their shade.
But truly, barred by lack of time, I pass this by
and leave it to be recounted by others after me.

Now come! I shall disclose the natural endowments that
Jupiter himself has given bees to reward them for   150
following the Cretans' melodic chords and clashing bronze
and nourishing the king of heaven in Mount Dicte's cave.
They alone hold their offspring in common, share the houses
of their city, and live out their lives under grand laws.
They alone know a fatherland as well as settled homes   155
and, aware of winter to come, they spend the warm weather
hard at work and, among themselves, put aside the profits.
For, some are vigilant to gather food and by fixed
agreement keep busy in the fields; others in the confines
of their homes put down the tears of narcissus and sticky gum   160
from tree bark as the first foundations of the comb, then
suspend wax that holds fast; some lead out the grown young,
hope of the species; others press together the purest
honey and cause the cells to bulge with liquid nectar;
there are those to whom it falls by lot to stand guard at the gates, 165
and they in turn observe the signs of rain and clouds in heaven
or take the burdens from arrivals or, troops drawn up,
keep the drones, a feckless bunch, away from the stalls.
The work glows, and fragrant honey releases the scent of thyme.
And just as the giant Cyclopes when they quickly forge   170
thunderbolts from malleable ore, some make gusts of air come

and go with ox-hide bellows, others plunge sizzling brass
into the lake; Mount Etna groans under the anvils placed on her;
by turns, with mighty force, they raise their arms in measured
rhythm and turn the iron with tongs that hold it fast: 175
not otherwise, if small may be compared to large,
an innate love of increase impels Athenian bees,
each at its own task. The elders care for the towns
both building honeycombs and forming intricate houses.
But late at night the weary young return, their legs laden   180
with thyme; they feed hither and thither on arbutus
and pale-green willow, on cassia, too, and ruddy crocus
and the resin-rich lime tree and the dark-blue hyacinth.
For all, there is a time to rest from work, for all a time to labor.
At daybreak they rush from the gates with no delay; later,   185
when Evening advises them to leave off feeding
in the fields, then they seek their homes, then they groom their
    bodies;
sound rises as they buzz around doorways and thresholds.
Later, when they've laid themselves in their chambers, silence
rules the night, and well-deserved sleep possesses their weary
    limbs.   190
Nor truly, when rain menaces, do they fly very far
from their stables or trust the sky when storms blow in from the
    east,
but all around, beneath their steep walls, they fetch water
and attempt short flights and, just as unstable skiffs take on
ballast when the sea is tossing, they lift up pebbles   195
to steady themselves amid the wispy clouds.

    You'll also note that this behavior has satisfied
the bees — they don't indulge in mating, not letting their bodies
go slack in love nor bringing forth their young with effort;

in truth, without male help, they themselves gather young in their
    mouths   200
from leaves, from sweet grass; they themselves supply the king
    and small
citizens and rebuild their castles, their waxen kingdoms.
Often, too, wandering amid hard rocks, they injure
their wings and, more than that, forfeit life under their loads,
so strong their love of flowers, their glory in making honey.   205
Therefore, though a short life limits each individual
bee, for it never lasts longer than the seventh summer,
the species remains immortal, and the fortune of the house
lasts many years, with ancestors' ancestors accounted for.

And more — not Egypt nor powerful Lydia, not the tribes   210
east of the Caspian Sea nor those near the Indus so honor
their king. When he is safe, all are of a single mind;
when he is gone, they break faith, they themselves pull down
the honey they've made and tear the caps off the comb.
He is the guardian of their work. They revere him, and all   215
surround him with a constant hum; great numbers attend him
and often lift him to their shoulders. For him they cast their
bodies in battle's way and seek a grand death from their wounds.

Having followed these signs and these habits, some say
that bees own a share of the divine soul and drink in   220
the ether of space; for, god invests everything —
earth and the tracts of the sea and deepest heaven;
from him, flocks, herds, men, all species of wild animals —
each one gains for itself at birth its little life;
doubtless, afterward, all return to him and, released, are   225
made new; death has no place but, alive, they fly up, each
to be counted as a star and ascend into heaven above.

Whenever you'd unseal their confined abode and the honey
stored in their treasury, first wet your mouth with water
and freshen it, and with your hand spread smoke that seeks them
    out.   230
Twice they gather the abounding produce, collection occurs two
    times:
as soon as one of the Pleiades has shown her fine face
to the earth and thrust away Ocean's stream with scornful foot,
and then when the same star, fleeing the rains of November,
has sadly descended from heaven into the wintry waves.   230   235
Their wrath is beyond measure; injured, they breathe poison
into the bites and, when they've attached to the vein, let loose
their invisible darts and surrender their lives in the wound.
But if you fear a hard winter and would preserve their future
pitying their bruised spirits and broken condition,   240
who indeed would pause before fumigating them with thyme
and cutting away empty cells? For, often the newt, out of sight,
eats at the combs, the chambers swarm with light-shunning beetles,
while the drone that does nothing sits down to food meant for
    others,
or the cruel hornet closes in on the bees' weaker weapons,   245
or moths, an ominous species, or the spider, hateful
to Minerva, hangs its loosely spun webs in the doorways.
The more they're emptied out, the more vigorously all will
work to repair the ruins of their fallen kind — filling in
the rows of cells and building their hives with flower juice.   250

Because life brings our misfortunes also to the bees,
truly, if their bodies languish from severe sickness,
this you can know from the first by undoubted symptoms:
their color changes at once with disease; an ugly
thinness deforms their looks; then they carry bodies devoid   255
of light from the house and lead sad funeral processions.

They may hang from the entrances joined at their feet
or linger within their closed dwelling, all of them
listless with hunger and numbed by shriveling cold.
Then, a heavier sound is heard, a slow susurration,   260
as sometimes the chilly South Wind whispers in the woods,
as the restless sea hisses when the waves recede,
as consuming fire sizzles in closed-up furnaces.
I'll advise you then to burn aromatic gum
and bring them honey through tubes made of reeds, cheering
    them   265
and calling those worn by disease to familiar food.
It would also help to mix the taste of pounded oak galls
and dried roses, or must boiled to richness over high flames,
or raisin wine made from bunches of dried Parthian grapes,
Attic thyme, as well, and centaury with a strong odor.   270
There is also a flower in the meadows, to which farmers
give the name starwort, a plant that's easily acquired,
for from one clump it raises a great forest of growth.
Golden, the disk itself, but in the petals, spread around
thickly, lavender highlights gleam amid dark violet.   275
Often, the altars of the gods are adorned with its braided wreaths;
it tastes bitter to the tongue; shepherds gather it in close-cropped
pastures and near the Mella's meandering stream.
Boil the roots of this plant in aromatic wine,
then set them out at the bees' doors in full baskets as food.   280

But if all of someone's stock has suddenly failed him
and he knows not whence to call the species back in a new line,
it's high time to tell of the Arcadian master's memorable
discovery and the way in which, often in those days,
the rotting blood of a slaughtered ox has brought forth bees.   285
I shall disclose everything, going back to the prime source.
For where the blessèd people of Egyptian Canopus

dwell by the still waters of the Nile in springtime flood
and sail around their fields in painted papyrus boats,
and where the border of quiver-bearing Persia presses close,   290
and where the rushing stream branches out in seven different   292
mouths, flowing down all the way from the dark-skinned Indians,   293
and makes green Egypt fruitful with its black mud,   291
the entire region entrusts its sure prosperity to this art.
First, small and restricted to this very use, a place   295
is selected; this they enclose with a narrow roof
of tiles and closely set walls; then away from the four
winds, add four windows with indirect light.
Next, a steer is sought, the horns on his two-year-old forehead
just arching up; both his nostrils and his breathing mouth are
   blocked,   300
despite his mighty struggles, and when he is killed by blows,
his flesh is pounded through the intact hide until it breaks down.
They leave him this way in the enclosure and scatter broken
twigs, thyme, and fresh-cut cassia beneath his flanks.
This is done when the West Wind first agitates the waves,   305
even before the meadows blush with spring colors, even
before the chittering barn swallow hangs her nest on the beams.
Meanwhile, the moisture stews, warmed in the softened
bones, and — look! — miraculous creatures, at first
without feet, but soon, wings eagerly buzzing, they   310
swarm together, taking more and more to the light air,
until, like rain pouring from the clouds of summer,
they burst forth, or like arrows from a twanging bowstring,
as when lightly armed Parthians first sally into battle.

    What god — Muses, tell me — hammered out this skill for us?   315
Whence rose this novel practice that caught our fancy?
The shepherd Aristaeus, leaving the Tempe valley
where Peneus flows, his bees lost — so legend reports — to sickness

and hunger, stopped, beset by sorrow, at the stream's holy
source and, loudly lamenting, called out to his mother,   320
"Mother, Cyrene, my mother, living beneath this gush
of water, why did you bear me from the radiant line
of gods — Apollo fathered me, if you've told the truth —
only to be scorned by fate? What has routed your love?
Why did you let me hope for immortality?   325
Look at me! Even this crowning grace of my human life
that zealous care for cattle and crops hammered out for me,
even though you are my mother, I give it all up.
Yes, come! With your own hand root out my fruit trees,
burn my livestock pens, murder my crops, torch my gardens,   330
chop my vines down with a battle-axe if you have been seized
by such great disdain for work that is well worth your praise.

    But his mother, in her palace below the river's deep bed,
has heard his cry. The Nymphs around her were carding Anatolian
fleeces dyed the rich color of bottle-green glass —   335
Woods Girl and Golden and Clear Voice and Fancy Leaf,
hair gleaming, loose-flowing over white shoulders;
[and Radiant and Sprightly and Festive and Wave-Catcher]
Proud Filly, too, along with Wolf-Eyes, the one a virgin,
the other new to childbirth's goddess-given pangs,   340
and Proclaimer, her sister Comet, both daughters of Ocean,
both decked with gold, both dressed for the hunt in decorated
    hides,
and Corinth and Awe and Divine Face from Asia,
and Arethusa, fleet huntress, her arrows at last laid aside.
Seated among them, famed Power told stories of Vulcan's   345
futile efforts, of Mars' deceit and stolen delights,
and, from Chaos on, detailed the busy love lives of the gods.
As they, enchanted by the tale, spun the soft yarn off
their spindles, Aristaeus' wailing battered again

at his mother's ears, and all, seated on thrones of clear glass,   350
started with surprise, till Arethusa, first of the sisters
to peek, raised her blonde head from the river's great waves
and called from the far air, "Cyrene, sister, not in vain
your alarm at such roaring. It's he, your greatest worry,
Aristaeus, downcast, tear-drenched as he stands at the brink   355
of our father's waters and curses your hard heart."
Her heart assailed by sudden fear, his mother cried out,
"Bring him down, bring him here. He's allowed to cross the
   threshold
of the gods." That instant she ordered the stream's deep waters
divide to give the young man a path. But the waves   360
curling in combers high as a mountain, surrounded him,
folded him into their vast embrace, and bore him deep down.
Amazed now by his mother's home, its sovereign waters
and cavern-locked lakes and rustling glades of river grass,
he moved along, and stunned by their prodigious rush,   365
he beheld all the rivers, both near and far, as they flowed
beneath the great earth—the Rion in Colchis, Phrygia's Wolf,
the Thessalian spring from which deep Enipeus first wells forth,
the source of Father Tiber, too, and fluent Anio,
of Europe's Bug, dashing over rocks, and Caicus in Asia,   370
of the bull-like Po, head crowned with two golden horns—
no river more forceful races through grain-laden fields
in its reckless thrust toward the blue-dark sea.
Soon as he came beneath the palace's domed roof of soft
volcanic stone, and Cyrene saw that her son wept   375
useless tears, her sisters in turn wash his hands with clean
water and bring in towels of closely shorn wool.
Some spread a feast on the table and keep the goblets full,
while altar fires are kindled with Arabian incense.
And his mother cries, "Take the cups of Lydian wine,   380
let us pour a libation to Ocean." Then she prays

to Ocean, the father of all things, and to the sister
Nymphs, who protect a hundred rivers and a hundred groves.
Three times she pours clear nectar on the hearth where holy fire
    burns,
three times the flickering flames blaze bright, reaching high to the
    roof,   385
an omen to buck up his spirits. She begins to speak:

    "In Neptune's fief, between Crete and Rhodes, dwells the seer
Proteus, blue-green as the sea, who harnesses steeds with horse-
forelegs and fishy tails to speed his chariot through the deeps.
Right now he cruises Macedonia's ports and Pallene,   390
his birthplace. We sister Nymphs and Nereus, old as time,
revere him, for everything comes to the seer —
all that is, all that has been, and all that shall come to pass.
For, Neptune has willed it so, whose stupendous herds
and rough-coated seals the seer pastures deep in the sea.   395
First, my son, you must bind him in shackles so that he
tells you what sickened the bees and puts the matter right.
Without force, he'll give no satisfaction, nor can you
bend him by pleading; with force unabated and shackles
take him captive. These will break his tricks to pieces.   400
And I myself, when the sun kindles its heat at high noon,
when grass droops with thirst, and the flock truly welcomes shade,
shall lead you to the hideaway, where, weary of the waves,
the old man comes ashore — easy to take him while he sleeps.
But, soon as you hold him fast with shackles and your hands,   405
a host of forms and feral shapes will seek to deceive you.
Lightning-quick, he'll turn into a bristling boar, a black tiger,
a scaly adder, a lioness with tawny neck,
or he'll burst into roaring flames and so slip through
his shackles or slide away as a dribble of water.   410
But, shape after shape, the more he transforms himself,

the more, my son, must you twist his shackles tight
till at last his body stops shifting and you see him
as you saw him first, his eyes closing as he fell asleep."

  She said this and poured a sweet stream of ambrosia,   415
massaging it over her son's entire body
till its airy fragrance breathed from his combed hair
and vigor returned to his arms and legs. There is a huge cave
scoured out of a mountainside, where a great wash of waves,
impelled by the wind, surges, then lapses into rivulets —   420
the safest haven, once, for storm-tossed mariners.
In there, Proteus takes shelter behind the barrier-rock.
And here the Nymph hides her son in a cranny away
from the light; then she stands back, concealed in a mist.
The Dog Star's fierce heat blazed in the heavens parching   425
all India, and the fiery sun had run half his course —
grasses were seared, and the streams, their throats dry,
ran low over beds that the sun's rays had baked —
when Proteus, seeking his favorite haunt, headed
out of the waves. Around him the sea-drenched tribes of vast
    ocean,   430
leaping in play, shook the salt spray far and wide from their pelts.
Seals stretched themselves out hither and yon to sleep on the shore.
He himself, like some herdsman high in the mountains,
when evening brings calves from pasture to barn
and lambs whet the hunger of wolves with their bleating,   435
sits in their midst on a boulder and counts every one.
The moment opportunity arrives, Aristaeus,
scarcely letting the old man rest his weary limbs, falls
upon him with a roar and fastens him in manacles
where he lies. The old man, forgetting nothing of his art,   440
transforms himself into an all-encompassing
array of shapes — fire and fearsome beast and flowing stream.
But when no stratagem delivers him, vanquished, he

resumes his own shape and speaks at last in a human voice:
"Who then, you young, most impudent upstart, has told you   445
to break and enter my home? What do you want here?" But he,
"You know, Proteus, you know full well. Nobody fools *you*.
So stop diddling *me*. Obeying the gods' instructions,
I come here looking for answers to explain my foul luck."
That's what he said. Then, the diviner, under great force,   450
rolled eyes that glittered with sea-blue light, and gritting
his teeth, opened his lips to release the truth.

"Nothing less than heaven's wrath chases you down. You pay
for enormous crimes. Orpheus, savage with mourning,
demands this punishment, less than you warrant had not fate   455
intervened. He grieves bitterly for his stolen wife.
Your fault! When she fled headlong at the river to escape your
advances, the poor girl did not see death lurking at her feet
in the high grass — the huge water snake that guards the
    streambanks.
Her friends, the Wood Nymphs, filled the high peaks with
    ululation,   460
and these wailed, too — the heights of Rose Mountain and the
    lofty
Whole-Earth range in Thrace, and King Rhesus' war-loving land,
and tribes on the Danube, rivers in Thrace, the North Wind's wife.
Orpheus, strumming his hollow-shell lyre to soothe his torn heart,
sang you, sweet wife, sang you to himself on the lonely shore,   465
day in, day out, sang you at sunrise, sang you at sunset.
The jaws of a Spartan cavern, Death's towering gateway,
and the grove miasmic with black dread — he entered them
and came to the realm of the dead with its fearsome king,
their hearts impossible to soften with living prayers.   470
But waked by the song, out of the abyss of Darkness,
the shades drifted up, slight apparitions devoid of light
and numberless as birds that find refuge in the leaves

when nightfall or a winter storm drives them from the hills —
mothers and men, the ghosts of great-hearted heroes,   475
their earthly lives over, and boys, unwed girls, and sons
placed on a funeral pyre as their parents looked on.
Surrounded by black slime and blighted reeds, they are trapped
in the sluggish flow of wailing Cocytus
while the hateful Styx prisons them within nine spirals.   480
Yes, the homeplace of Death and the farthest crannies of Hell
were stunned by the song; the Furies, too, their hair entangled
with bile-green snakes, and Cerberus's three jaws fell agape,
while the wind-driven wheel of Ixion came to a dead stop.
Now, heading home, he had escaped all misfortune,   485
and his Eurydice, restored, approached the upper air
following him (as Proserpina had stipulated),
when a sudden madness swept through the incautious lover,
forgivable — if only the Dead knew how to forgive.
He stopped and on the very brink of light looked back on his   490
Eurydice — a mindless act, his goal annulled. That instant
his hard work emptied out, the agreement with brutal Death
shattered. Three times thunder crashed over Averno's swamps.
'Orpheus,' she cried, 'what terrible folly has brought perdition
to you and hapless me? Look! Again the merciless   495
Fates call me back, and sleep seals my eyes, swimming with tears.
Farewell. I am taken back now, cloaked in the night, and, oh,
reaching out to you with powerless hands that are no longer yours.'
She said this and faded that instant away
from his sight like smoke blending into thin air   500
and no longer saw him as he grasped at the shadows
with much he still wanted to say. Nor did Death's ferryman
let him cross again the swamp that separated them.
What could he do? Where go, his wife twice stolen from him?
Could tears persuade ghosts, or pleading, Hell's numinous
    powers?   505

Death-cold, she now floated away in the hateful black boat.
They say that for seven months uninterrupted,
beneath a cliff towering over a desolate Thracian stream,
he wept and, shivering under the stars, sang this song,
gentling tigers and enticing the oaks to dance.   510
He sang as the nightingale sings from the shade
of a poplar lamenting her lost chicks that a hard-hearted
ploughboy, spotting the nest, has taken before they fledged;
she weeps all night and, perched on a branch, repeats her sad
song, filling the night far and wide with her sorrowful plaint.   515
Not Love herself nor any thoughts of marriage could bend his
    heart.
Alone he wandered the frozen north, the ice-locked river Don,
and snow-clad mountains by the Black Sea, ever bereft,
lamenting his stolen Eurydice and Death's
voided gift. But Thracian women, riled by his heedlessness   520
invading their nocturnal rites, their god-drunken revels,
ripped his young body to pieces and flung them hither and yon.
But even when the river Hebrus that flowed through his
father's kingdom rolled his head, torn from its marble neck,
tumbling it midstream, the voice and the cold tongue kept singing   525
with fading breath, Eurydice, oh poor Eurydice!
'Eurydice,' echoed the banks down the river's length."

    So Proteus said and, spinning around, dived into the depths,
and where he dived, a whirlpool lathered the water with spume.
But Cyrene stepped forth and spoke to the startled young man: 530
"My son, let go of the cares that have brought you sorrow.
Here is the whole cause of sickness: it came from the Nymphs
with whom she once danced beneath tall trees in the sacred groves.
They thrust this heartbreaking ruin upon your bees. Make
peace offerings, show reverence to the holy women of the
    woods —   535

they'll readily grant forgiveness to prayers, they'll let anger go.
But first I'll tell you how you must present your plea.
Four prime bulls of the best conformation — choose them
from your herd now grazing in the high green mountain pastures
of Arcadia, and as many heifers with necks never yoked.   540
Four altars — for your cleansing, build them on the goddesses'
time-old shrines, and drain the sacrificial blood from the throats
of the cattle but let their bodies stay in the leafy grove.
Nine days later, when Dawn brings sunrise, you must give
Orpheus the poppies of forgetfulness that he is due,   545
then sacrifice a black ewe and revisit the grove.
There, Eurydice appeased, venerate her, killing a calf."
No dallying, he obeys her commands to the last word.
He comes to the shrines, erects the altars as instructed.
Four prime bulls of the best conformation — he leads them   550
there, and as many heifers with necks never yoked.
Nine days later, when Dawn brings in the sunrise, he pays
his dues to Orpheus and revisits the grove.
Here, a sudden omen, plain to see, almost incredible
to tell: out of the putrefying bovine guts, out   555
of the bellies and burst sides, bees, buzzing, swarming,
then streaming upward in huge clouds till they join in a tree-
top and hang in a great ball from a bending branch.

     This I sang over and above the care of fields and herds,
over and above the care of trees, while great Caesar's lightning   560
struck in war by the deep Euphrates and he, as victor, gave
laws to eager peoples and gained the path to Olympus.
In those days, sweet Naples nourished me — Virgil —
who flourished at leisure in undistinguished efforts,
I who played with shepherds' songs and, as a bold youth, sang   565
you, Tityrus, under the leafy crown of a spreading beech.

NOTES TO THE TRANSLATION

THE NOTES ARE KEYED TO THE LINE NUMBERS OF THE ENGLISH TEXT.

BOOK ONE

The first book of the poem focuses on planting and harvesting crops and the astronomical events that signal what to do and when to do it. The farmer's seasonal tasks are described, along with his tools.

1–42: The proem. Lines 1–4 introduce the subjects of the four books: crops, trees and vines, livestock, and bees. Lines 5–42 comprise a prayer for the poem's success, with lines 5–24 invoking deities associated with rural life and lines 25–42 addressed to Octavian, soon to become Augustus Caesar and destined after death to take his deserved place in the heavenly pantheon.

1: Each of the poem's four books addresses Maecenas, Virgil's patron, who served as a minister to Octavian, later to be Augustus Caesar. Placed in charge of distributing literary patronage, he was also a patron of the poet Horace (65–8 B.C.). Virgil's first mention of Maecenas occurs here.

7: The Italic god whom Virgil invokes is Liber, here translated as "old Planter God." Ceres is the goddess in whose care reside the planting of crops and their harvest.

8: Virgil's "Chaonian acorns" here become simply "wild acorns." The Chaonian district lies in Epirus in Greece and was the site of an oracle devoted to Zeus. According to the poet, acorns served as human food in the preagricultural age.

9: The river named here is the Greek Achelous.

10–11: The "guardian Gods of Fields and Folds" are the Fauns, old Italic deities; the "Tree Nymphs" are Dryads. Both are associated in the Roman mind with shepherds' work.

14–15: These lines refer to Aristaeus, who will figure importantly in book IV as a farmer who loses, then magically regenerates, his bees. In a convention of Virgil's time, the name is not used, and the ancient reader/listener would infer it from the mention of Keos, here translated as "the Cyclades."

16–18: Pan, invoked here as *Tegeaee* — spirit of the Arcadian town of Tegea — is asked to come from *Maenalus,* a range of mountains in Arcadia.

19: The young man, not named here, is Triptolemus, given seed grain and a plow by Demeter, who sent him around the world in a chariot drawn by snakes so that he could teach the arts of agriculture to humankind.

20: Silvanus was an Italic god associated with forests and uncultivated land.

30: Ultima Thule is a classic phrase that retains to this day its ancient reference to the northernmost inhabitable place.

33–35: Virgil proposes that Octavian might choose to occupy the heavenly space in which Libra is found.

38: The reference here to Proserpina foreshadows her mention in book IV, line 487.

41–42: In speaking of "country people unaware of their way," Virgil asks for a revitalization of agriculture and a return to family farming, which had been severely disrupted by civil wars and massive dispossession when rural land was seized as payment for veterans.

43–70: These lines deal with preparing the land for crops by plowing.

56–59: In these lines Virgil's knowledge of far-flung people and places first asserts itself. "Asia Minor" translates Virgil's *Tmolus,* a mountain in ancient Lydia which was situated in western Asia Minor. "Arabians" translates Virgil's *Sabaei,* Sabaeans, who lived in southwestern Arabia. "Soft" indicates their supposed effeminacy. The "Black Sea" translates *Chalybes,* a steel-making people who lived on the sea's south shore. As for beaver oil, *castoreum,* it is a malodorous substance found in glands in a beaver's groin area; it was used medicinally in Virgil's day.

61: Prometheus's son is named in the text: Deucalion.

68: The rising of Arcturus in early September presages bad weather.

77–99: These lines describe the care of the soil: letting land lie fallow, weed removal, crop rotation, enriching the soil with manure and ashes, burning off stubble, and finally, hoeing, dragging, and cross-plowing the fields.

78: The text reads "the poppies of Lethe," naming one of Hades' rivers. Drinking its water induced forgetfulness.

100–17: Here Virgil treats of irrigation and drainage.

102: "Anatolia's Aegean coast" translates *Mysia,* an ancient country located in northwestern Anatolia with coasts on both the Aegean and the Sea of Marmara.

103: "mountains inland" translates *Gargara,* a peak in the Ida range located in central Anatolia.

118–46: The subject of these lines is Jupiter's introduction of agriculture and its never-ending work into human life, which hitherto had known only a golden age in which "Earth herself gave everything more freely when no one made demands." Here Virgil first sounds the poem's insistence on *labor,* the unremitting effort that must go into farming if it is to be a success. But even with hard work success is not assured.

120: "Eurasian cranes" translates *Strymoniae grues,* Strymonian cranes. The Strymon, the modern Struma, is a river on the border of Thrace and Macedonia. Eurasian crane is the present-day common name of the species that has ever been seen in that part of the world.

121: "The Father himself" is Jupiter, also known as Jove.

125: "Before Jove took power" refers to a mythic golden age in which Saturn reigned, and living was not encumbered by the need to work.

138: "the princess whom Jove turned into the bright Bear" is named in the text as "Lycaon's daughter," otherwise known as Callisto.

147–59: The goddess Ceres introduces agriculture, an art which is soon beset by enemies, like weeds, seed-devouring birds, and drought.

149: The "holy oak groves" refer indirectly to Dodona in Greece, site of a shrine sacred to Zeus. The oak trees there provided roosts for doves, whose cooing, thought to be oracular, was interpreted by priestesses, themselves called doves.

153: Darnel is considered poisonous because it can cause dizziness if eaten.

160–75: These lines describe the implements—"the weapons"—with which the farmer can vanquish his enemies: grain cart, sledge, drag, hoe, items made of wicker, winnow, and, most important, the plow.

163: The text names the "Eleusinian mother," Demeter, who is Ceres' Greek counterpart. It refers to the rites performed in Demeter's honor at Eleusis.

165–66: Just as grain carts are ascribed to Demeter, wickerware comes from the mythic Greek king Celeus and the winnow from the god Iacchus, who seems to have personified the cries of the celebrants of the Eleusinian rites. Both king and god were associated with Demeter's rites. Iacchus has also been identified as a counterpart of Bacchus.

169–75: These lines give the only surviving description of a Roman plow. What an actual plow looked like is still open to conjecture, but from this account, it would have been a sturdy, durable implement.

176–203: This portion of the poem deals with rules of thumb to guide the farmer's constant battle with natural forces—weeds, destructive mammals, amphibians, and insects. It surveys such matters as the proper preparation of a threshing floor, predicting the harvest of grain, the treatment of seeds before planting, and selecting seeds for sowing in the year to come.

199–203: These lines comment on entropy. Even the hardest work is not always enough to keep nature at bay. Yet the human obligation under the Jovian regime is to keep on doing our best.

204–30: Here Virgil sets out the astronomical signs for plowing and sowing.

204–5: Arcturus and Auriga rise in spring and set in October. Draco does not set.

217–18: In April, Taurus rises and the Dog Star, Canis, sets.

221–22: Virgil seems to suggest late autumn. The Pleiades set in mid-November, and Corona, in mid-December. The text calls the Pleiades *Eoae Atlantides,* the "dawn-daughters of Atlas," a roundabout way of saying that the Pleiades set in the morning. "Cretan star" translates *Cnosia,* the star of Knossos. It refers to Ariadne, daughter of King Minos of Crete, famous for Minos's bull, the Minotaur. At death she was transformed by Zeus into the brightest star in the constellation Corona Borealis.

225: Maia is one of the Pleiades.

231–56: Virgil describes the five zones of the world and the ways in which humankind can use their signs to zero in on the proper times for sowing and harvest, going to sea, launching a fleet, and felling ships' timbers.

240: Instead of "the north's Caucasian peaks," the text names Scythia and Riphaeus. Scythia is an ancient country bounded on the south by the Caspian Sea and Riphaeus, a mythic mountain range in the farthest north. It was later relocated in Scythia.

242–43: While Virgil rightly places one pole at the far northern top of the earth, he oddly but not illogically sets the southern pole below earth's surface.

253–56: Here Virgil conjoins references to farming and seafaring, both of which need to be fully aware of astronomical signs.

257–75: These lines depict the work to be done during the winter and bad weather. Even on holy days, a farmer is permitted to labor.

265: The text reads *Amerina retinacula,* "Amerian ties." Amerina was an Umbrian town apparently well endowed with willows, the limber twigs of which were used for tying up grapevines.

276–86: Here Virgil, listing propitious and ill-omened days for work, consciously pays homage to the Greek poet Hesiod (flourished about 800 B.C.), who wrote *Works and Days,* a didactic poem on farming. See note to II.176.

277: The text reads *pallidus Orcus,* "pallid Orcus." Orcus is the name of a god of the underworld; he personifies death.

278–80: The text may be translated literally as "Earth with unholy birth pangs bore Coeus and Iapetus and savage Typhoeus and the brothers who plotted to overthrow heaven." Coeus and Iapetus were Titans; Iapetus fathered Prometheus, Epimetheus, and Atlas. Typhoeus was a monster, whose many hands were snake heads and whose body from the waist down was nothing but snakes. The brothers, not named in the text, were Otus and Ephialtes, sons of Aloeus and Iphimedia rather than Earth. In the story of piling Ossa on Pelion, Virgil follows Homer, not Hesiod.

287–310: The first twelve lines of this portion treat of the kinds of work best done in the cool of night or in midday heat; the next twelve lines, with work in cold weather. The images here are truly vivid.

302–4: Again, Virgil makes a comparison between agricultural and nautical life.

309: The Balearic Islands include Majorca, Minorca, and Ibiza, in the western Mediterranean off the east coast of Spain.

311–50: Despite his unremitting work, the farmer is ever subject to the vagaries of nature. Here Virgil brings on a storm of inhuman proportions. Its "black whirlwind," its thunderstorms, its soaking rains and hard gales all suggest the civil strife that battered Rome for the first two-thirds of the first century B.C.

332: The text names Rhodope, a mountain range in western Thrace, and Ceraunia, a range in the Caucasus.

337: The text reads *ignis Cyllenius*, "Cyllenian fire," here translated as "Mercury's fire." Cyllenian refers to Mount Cyllene in Arcadia, where the god Mercury was said to have been born.

351–463: This portion of book I treats of signs for reading the weather.

351–92: These lines give the signs for forecasting high winds, rainstorms, and other kinds of bad weather. Some signs are astronomical; others are given by such terrestrial creatures as birds and ants.

384: The river named in the text is *Caystros*, the Cayster, an Anatolian river noted for its population of swans.

393–423: These lines list signs for forecasting "sunny days with clear skies." Again, in addition to astronomical phenomena, birds and terrestrial events are used as indicators.

398–409: Virgil may have played with these lines, which seem characterized by patterned line endings. This effect may be accidental, but it is too prominent to leave unattended in the translation. It is strongest in lines 398–409. The Latin endings of the first eight lines are *–unt, -os, -os, -unt, -o, -us, -us, -o*. The next four lines repeat words: *pinnis, auras, auras, pinnis*.

398: Thetis, foremost of the sea-dwelling Nereids, was the mother of Achilles. The bird named in the text is the mythical halcyon, which was thought to be able to calm the sea in winter for fourteen days; during that time, it made its nest and raised its young at sea. The halcyon's earthly counterpart is the kingfisher, a bird that lives at the verge of water and soil.

404–9: These lines recount the myth of Nisus and his daughter Scylla. Nisus, a king ruling on the Isthmus of Corinth, possessed a lock of red hair that kept safe both his throne and his life. King Minos from Crete laid siege to Nisus's territory, and Scylla, beholding him, fell in love. To ensure his victory over her father, she cut off Nisus's magical lock. In death Nisus was transformed into a sea hawk, and his daughter, jilted by Minos, into the mythical *ciris,* a small bird with an iridescent white body and coral feet.

424–37: Here Virgil gives instruction on signs given by the moon.

429: Again, an astronomical sign, this one given by the moon, is of interest to both farmer and sailor.

430–31: Virgil calls the moon *aurea Phoebe,* "golden Phoebe," who may spread "a virginal rosiness over her face." The reference here is clearly to the virgin goddess Diana, who is associated with the moon.

437: Virgil simply lists Glaucus, Panopea, and Ino's Melicertes, the last being the son of Ino, daughter of Cadmus, who founded Thebes. The adjectives appended to each name in the English translation reflect the meanings of the names.

438–60: Signs given by the sun are described.

463–514: The book rolls tumultuously to its conclusion by describing the signs and portents that presaged or accompanied civil war and the assassination of Julius Caesar in 44 B.C. Virgil's list of portents comprises the most extensive found in any ancient writer. They include sun signs, warnings from dogs and birds, volcanic eruptions, thunderstorms that sound like clashing armaments, earthquakes, livestock speaking, ivory statues in the temples shedding tears, bronze images sweating, and the appearance of "ominous threads" in the entrails of sacrificed animals. The long list is enough to make even modern readers shudder. This whole section foreshadows the plagues described at the end of book III.

472–73: Virgil writes here of the "ruptured furnaces" of the *Cyclopes,* the mythical giants who were said to have worked at their forges within Sicily's Mount Etna.

474: Germany, bordering on Gaul and fully aware of the civil conflicts roiling Rome, posed a threat to the moribund Roman Republic.

481: Virgil refers to the Po by its ancient name, *Eridanus.*

489–90: There was, in fact, only one battle at Philippi, fought in 42 B.C., in which the Triumvirate of Octavian, Mark Antony, and the general Marcus Lepidus defeated their chief opponents, Cassius and Brutus, the conspirators behind Julius Caesar's assassination. The other battle to which Virgil seems to refer was that at Pharsalus, 48 B.C., when Julius Caesar vanquished Pompey. The two events, one reminiscent of the other, both occurred in Macedonia, although certainly not in the same place.

491–92: The places named by Virgil are Emathia, a poetic word for the whole of Macedonia, and Haemus, a mountain range in the present-day Balkans.

499–500: The text gives the "young man's hilltop abode" as *Palatium,* the Palatine, one of Rome's famed seven hills. The young man, not named in the text, is, of course, Octavian.

502: Laomedon, king of Troy and father of Priam, promised payment to Apollo and Poseidon for their help in building the city's walls but reneged when the job had been done. This act led the outraged gods to support the Greek forces during the Trojan War. The idea of guilt having to be expiated in bloody internecine strife by generation after generation occurs elsewhere in Latin thinking: Aeneas's desertion of the Carthaginian queen Dido, for example, was thought to have incited the Punic Wars.

501–3: Describing abandoned farms, Virgil wrote from experience.

509: Both Assyria and Germany are here seen as fomenting war against Rome.

512–14: The book ends with a fast-paced simile comparing a world raging with war to a chariot drawn by out-of-control horses despite the driver's best attempts to slow them down.

BOOK TWO

This book surveys vegetation, trees and grapevines in particular.

1–8: The proem, invoking Bacchus, offers him a joyful invitation.

4, 7: The epithet applied to Bacchus here is *pater Lenaee,* "father of the winepress," a word which refers to the vat in which stomping, or treading, expresses the juice from the grapes.

7: Technically, the footgear that Bacchus is asked to pull off is his *coturni,* his "buskins," a thick-soled, laced boot that reached halfway to the knees. Such boots were worn by the actors in Greek and Roman tragedies. Because Bacchus is the god presiding over tragedy, it is fitting that he wears its style of boots.

9–34: This section deals with trees, those that volunteer naturally and those that men propagate by various methods.

16: "the oak that Greeks think capable of prophecy" refers to the oaks at Dodona, the shrine sacred to Zeus. See note to I.149.

18: For "Apollo's bay laurel," the Latin reads *Parnasia laurus,* "bay laurel of Mount Parnasus." Parnasus, on a flank of which Delphi was built, was a site sacred to Apollo.

35–46: The first four lines urge the farmer to learn all he can about farming. The next eight lines invoke Maecenas, Virgil's patron, and ask for his support in the current endeavor.

37–38: The names used by Virgil are Ismara, a mountain in Thrace, and Taburna, an Italian mountain. Ismara was notable for its wines, Taburna, for its olives.

39: Virgil again bows to his patron, Maecenas.

47–82: Lines 47–72 deal with the spontaneous propagation of trees in the wild and the necessary work that must go into domesticating them for human use. Lines 73–82 treat of grafting and transplanting.

61–62: The poem's central theme, the necessity for unremitting hard work, is clearly stated here.

66: Two legends associate Hercules with the poplar tree. One has it that Hercules made himself a crown of poplar leaves after he had brought the dog Cerberus up from Hades, the other simply that he brought the white poplar to Greece after finding it in Thesprotis, a region now part of Albania.

66–67: Virgil writes *Chaoniique patris glandes,* "acorns from a Chaonian father." Chaonia was the district in Epirus in which Dodona, dedicated to Zeus, was located. See notes to I.149 and II.16.

69–72: Only one of these grafts is actually possible, that of chestnut and beech, which belong to the same botanical family. Unrelated species cannot be successfully grafted. No matter: Virgil's pictures are truly marvelous.

73–82: Two methods are here explicated—grafting by budding and grafting by setting in slips.

83–108: A rhapsody on vines and on trees, especially those that bear fruit. Virgil lovingly, and very selectively, lists some varieties of grapes and the wines they produce.

85–86: Testicle-shaped olives are round, and shuttle-shaped olives, oblong. The "bitter-berried sort" was a variety picked early and thus not entirely ripe.

87: The text reads *Alcinoi silvae,* the "woods of Alcinous." Alcinous, mentioned by Homer, was a king famed for his gardens, which featured orchards that bore fruit year round.

91: Virgil writes *Thasiae vites et Mareotides albae,* "Thasian vines and pale [grapes] from Lake Mareia." Thasos is an island in the northern Aegean; Lake Mareia lies in Egypt.

96: Virgil writes *Rhaetica,* referring to the Rhaetian Alps just north of Verona, a region famed in those days for its vineyards. Later in the same line, turning to Italian wines, he mentions *cellis Falernis,* "Falernian cellars." The secrets of making Falernian wine, famed in Virgil's day, have long been lost, but we do know that it was made in Falernus, a district in the northern part of Campania.

97: Virgil writes *Aminneae vites,* "Aminnean vines," which were grown in Umbria, a now landlocked region that then stretched eastward to Italy's central Adriatic coast.

98: Virgil writes *Tmolius* and *Phanaeus,* referring to Tmolian and Phanean wines. The former came from Lydia, a country located in western Anatolia. The latter was made on the island of Chios, which lies just off the Anatolian coast.

99: Virgil names *argitis,* a variety of vine that produced white grapes.

109–35: Just as Virgil lists various species of trees in earlier sections, here, with equal selectivity, he lists various vegetable products harvested in exotic places, including India, Ethiopia, and China.

115: Here, "tattooed tribes north of the Caspian" translates *pictosque Gelonos.* The Geloni were a tribe native to Scythia, now Ukraine.

117: Virgil writes that frankincense belongs only to the Sabaeans, a people of southwest Arabia. See note to I.56–59.

119: Here, his nearly encyclopedic knowledge lapsing, Virgil names berries, not pods. Acacias, however, do not produce berries.

120: Virgil is clearly writing about cotton, a product for which the Latin of his time had no word. He imagines it growing on trees rather than in fields.

121: Virgil mentions the *Seres,* a people living east of Scythia and India — the Chinese, who were known for sericulture. Knowing nothing of how silk was actually produced by unraveling the cocoons of silkworms, Virgil and some of his contemporaries imagined that it was obtained by combing the leaves of a certain kind of tree.

136–76: This passage contains the famous *laudes Italiae,* the praises of Italy. Lines 136–42 contrast Virgil's native environment to those of foreign lands and finds them lacking. Lines 143–76 treat of the land's features and products, including livestock, and make no slight mention of man-made features, like cities. Virgil also calls a roster of the names of the great men of his time. And he presents here a rosy picture of the fruits of hard work.

136: The text names not Persia but Media, a land that occupied part of present-day Iran.

137: The river named here is the Hermus, situated in Lydia, now present-day Anatolia, or Asia Minor.

138: In the text "the Afghans' land" is the Parthian province Bactra, which occupied territory in present-day Afghanistan.

139: The "fabled place" is Panchaia, an imaginary land set in the Indian Ocean.

140–41: As two of the conditions for regaining the golden fleece, Jason yoked the wild bulls to a plow and sowed the dragon's teeth, whereupon a crop of armed men rose from the ground brandishing their weapons.

143–50: These lines review the subjects of books I–III: crops, trees and vines, and livestock.

143: Virgil writes *Bacchi Massicus umor,* "Bacchus's Massic liquid." Campania's Mount Massicus, now Monte Massico, was famed for its vineyards and wines.

149–54: Virgil exaggerates both climate and the productivity of cows and fruit trees. He looks back here to the golden Saturnian age, when living was easy.

150: The claim that cows bear calves twice each year and fruit trees yield twice each year is a fiction, of course, like that found at IV.121, which claims that the rose beds of Paestum bloom twice yearly.

155–57: The cities and towns are products of the Jovian era, which demands hard work from humankind.

158: Virgil writes of *mare supra* and *mare infra,* "the sea above" and "the sea below," respectively, the Adriatic on Italy's east coast and the Tuscan, or Tyrrhenian, on the west.

159–60: For Virgil's *Larus* and *Benacus,* the modern names are used, Como and Garda, respectively. Garda, the largest lake in Italy, is situated some twenty miles north of Virgil's hometown, Mantua.

161: Lake Lucrino, *Lucrinus* in the text, is more properly a saltwater lagoon belonging to the ancient resort town of Baiae in Campania on the Tuscan Sea. It was famed for its oysters.

164: Lake Averno, *Avernus* in the text, is also situated on the Campanian coast. Because its foul vapors were thought to kill birds, it became associated with death and was considered a portal to the underworld.

167–68: The text names the Marsi, the Sabelli, a Ligurian, and the Volsci. The Marsi and Sabelli, peoples living in the hills of central Italy, were Rome's fierce opponents in the Social War (90–89 B.C.), in which Italians who had not been granted Roman citizenship fought for independence from the Roman state. Liguria, home of present-day Genoa, is a coastal region in the piedmont of the Maritime Alps. The Volsci were an ancient Italic people who submitted to Roman rule at the end of the fourth century B.C. and subsequently became assimilated.

169–70: The praises of Italy move into the political arena. Victory, whether over the recalcitrant soil or over alien peoples, is bought through the hard work that subjugates both.

173–74: Virgil again makes note of the "land of Saturn," a Golden Age ideal.

176: "Hesiod's song" is *Works and Days,* probably composed during or slightly after Homeric days. Didactic in nature, it posits a golden age superseded by other ages, in which Zeus commands men to work hard and without cease. Instructing farmers in astronomical signs and seasonal tasks, making implements, building barns, planting crops and vineyards, harvesting, and similar farmwork, it served in many ways as a model for Virgil. But Virgil, cynical about the usefulness of worship and prayer, does not display Hesiod's stern piety.

177–225: These lines deal with various types of soil and the plants or animals that each best nurtures.

181: The text refers to Palladian olives — that is, olives associated with Pallas Athena, whose Roman counterpart was the goddess Minerva.

193: The text names *pinguis Tyrrhenus*, "fat Etruscan," who may not have been a priest but certainly played a ceremonial role at a sacrifice.

194: The "steaming organ meats" were the only part of the sacrifice not eaten by the congregants.

197: Taranto, *Tarentum* in the text, was famous for its fine sheep.

198: The reference to Mantua's lost plain harks back to Virgil's native town and the fact that many of its residents lost their land when Octavian settled decommissioned soldiers there in payment for their services.

207–11: Here the violence wrought by farmwork against nature receives a telling picture — the forests cut down, its birds gone.

225: "Campania's flooding river" is named in the text: Clanius, which frequently caused springtime flooding in the Campanian town of Acerrae.

226–58: These lines give advice on how to determine soil types by testing.

229: The "Body-Relaxer" is *Lyaeus*, a vivid surname of Bacchus. The word comes from the Greek verb *luo*, which means, among other things, "loosen," "unfold," "slacken," and "relax."

259–87: The lines treat first of preparing the soil for a vineyard, then of planting and training the vines.

266: This line gives the original meaning of the phrase "grape arbor" — a tree (usually an elm or an oak) for which the Latin word is *arbor*.

277–78: The picture here is one of each vine-supporting tree at the center of a square formed by footpaths. The subsequent lines illustrate the picture with a military simile.

288–97: These lines describe the depth at which to plant both vines and their supporting trees, especially the oak.

298–314: This portion of the poem contains prohibitions: do not do this, do not do that, culminating with advice on preventing fires.

315–45: These lines give advice on when to plow and when to plant. They culminate with a beautifully sensual celebration of spring, the season of the divine marriage of Sky and Earth, which Virgil imagines as having occurred from time immemorial.

336–42: These lines first hark back to the supposed golden age and its ever-temperate climate, then look at the necessity for respite from "bitter cold and searing heat" in the age of labor.

346–53: Here the lines treat of manuring, draining, and protecting plants.

354–61: This section gives advice on cultivation, plowing, and preparing trellises of poles and stakes to train the vines before they gain enough growth to climb rapidly up their supporting trees — their arbors, Latin *arbores*. In actuality, vines that bore grapes for making wine were not transplanted but tied directly to their trees.

362–70: Pruning — when to hold back, when to cut — is discussed here.

371–96: This section deals with protecting vines from heat and cold and from domestic sheep, heifers, and goats. Because of the damage they do, goats are sacrificed to Bacchus. Plays are traditionally performed at his festivals.

380–96: Virgil here transfers Greek practices related to the worship of Dionysos — the sacrifice of a goat, the performance of tragedies, rustic revelry — to Italy, where such things did not occur. His aim, however, is to focus on Bacchus, Dionysos's Roman equivalent, who is the deity presiding over this book.

380–81: Here Virgil seems to investigate the question of the origins of Greek tragedy, the Greek word for which translates as "goat song."

382: "Theseus' sons" are the Greeks, Theseus being the mythical founder of Athens. The origin of comedy given here is a supposition. To this day it is not clear how comedy arose. Nonetheless, Virgil's images are filled with vitality.

389–92: Hanging such wooden heads was thought to ensure fertility; thus, the abundance in lines 390–92.

393: "Our country's songs" is a gloss for Virgil's *Georgics*.

397–419: Virgil gives further instruction on the incessant human labor needed for successful viticulture: hoeing, pruning, weeding, dressing the vines, and worrying without cease about random assaults from the natural world. The passage is full of imperatives.

407: "Saturn's curved pruning hook" recalls the Greek myth of the Titan Cronus, with whom pre-Jovian Saturn may be identified. The story has it that Cronus castrated his father, Uranus, with a flint sickle.

412–13: Here Virgil neatly reverses one of Hesiod's maxims, W.D., 463: "Praise a small ship but put your cargo in a big one."

420–25: Here Virgil asserts that, unlike grapes, olives need little care.

426–57: This section treats of other trees and their products.

426–30: The lines recall the Saturnian dreamtime, in which the natural world took care of itself with little help from men.

433: This line is, in all probability, not Virgil's but an interpolation.

437–38: The text names Cytorus, a mountain in Anatolia, and Narycia, a town in the toe of Italy's boot, a region then known as Bruttium but now as Calabria.

448: The text refers to Ituraean bows. The Ituraeans were a people living in what is now Syria.

455–57: Once upon a time out of time, the Centaurs were guests at the wedding of Pirithous, a Lapith, and Hippodameia. They became so drunk that they made insulting advances to the bride, whereupon, in Virgil's version of the tale, the Lapiths took lethal revenge. Three Centaurs are named here: Rhoetus, Pholus, and Hylaeus. Of Rhoetus, nothing more is known. Ixion, eternally tortured in Hades by being strapped to a revolving wheel, fathered Pholus. Hylaeus attempted to rape Atalanta as she hunted a destructive boar, but she shot him through with an arrow.

458–540: In this famous passage, Virgil sings praise for the peaceful and pious life of a smallholder, who is portrayed as enjoying an almost Saturnian richesse in the age of labor.

473–74: The lines contain another evocation of the Saturnian golden age, a time when Justice, now absent, prevailed.

475–94: From "nature's farthest reaches" to "rural land and streams," Virgil surveys the possible subjects for his poems.

476: Here the poet represents himself as a priest of the Muses.

487–88: The text names Spercheus, a Thessalian river, and Taygetus, a Spartan range.

489: The text names Haemus, a mountain range in the area now known as the Balkans.

497: The "wild tribes" are those of the Dacians, a people living near the river Hister, the name given by the Romans to the lower Danube.

508–10: At least temporarily, popular statesmen could set aside the conflicts between the senate's aristocrats and the other classes of citizens. For decades, until the advent of Octavian, such conflicts had marked Virgil's life.

532–40: Virgil looks back in three successive stages, first to the Sabines, next to their predecessors Romulus and Remus, and last to Saturn's golden age, which ended when Ceres introduced agriculture.

536: Jupiter is not named in the text. He is rather referred to as Dicte's king. Myth has it that Jupiter was reared on Mount Dicte in Crete.

BOOK THREE

This book deals with the rearing and breeding of livestock, especially horses, cattle, sheep, and goats. The last portion treats of the random disasters with which nature willy-nilly afflicts farmers no matter how hard they work.

1–48: These lines comprise book III's proem. The first two invoke deities. In lines 3–9, Virgil rejects common, hackneyed subjects in favor of his present enterprise. In grand Pindaric fashion, Virgil uses lines 10–36 to build a temple, in which Caesar (Octavian) stands at the center. There, Virgil would award prizes to the winners of races and boxing matches. And he decorates the doors of the temple with scenes showing Octavian's victories in India, the Middle East, and the Mediterranean. Maecenas is then acknowledged just before the poet sets off on his quest to complete the *Georgics* and assure praise for Octavian.

1–2: The "Goddess of Shepherds" is Pales, an indigenous Roman deity. As for Apollo, the text names *pastor ab Amphryso*, "the shepherd from Amphrysus," Amphrysus being a river in Thessaly, where Apollo once served King Admetus, husband of Alcestis, as a shepherd. Pan, not named in the text, is referred to indirectly in the phrase *silvae amnesque Lycaei*, "woods and streams of Lycaeus," an Arcadian mountain sacred to Pan.

4–5: The text names both Eurystheus, the king in Argos who assigned twelve labors to Hercules, and the Egyptian king Busiris, given to sacrificing every stranger who came his way. Busiris was the brother of Antaeus, whom Hercules killed by holding him in the air so that he could not regain strength by touching his mother, Earth.

6–8: As "Hercules' lost friend," the text names Hylas, a beautiful boy who sailed with him and the other Argonauts on their search for the golden fleece. Hylas was seduced by water nymphs and taken to live in the grotto under their pool. "Latona's Delos," a literal translation of the Latin, refers to the island on which Latona gave birth to Apollo. "The bride Centaurs fought for" is Hippodameia, named here in the text (see II.455–57). Pelops, husband of Hippodameia, was, as a baby, cooked and served to the gods by his father, Tantalus; after eating his shoulder, the gods realized what they were doing and replaced the missing joint with a piece of ivory.

11: Virgil writes that he will lead the Muses from Aonia, the district in Boeotia in which Mount Helicon, long considered sacred to the Muses, is situated.

12: The text cites palms from Idumea, a Roman name for Palestine or Judea.

14: The Mincio, Latin *Mincius,* is a tributary of the Po, which flows from Lake Garda.

19: Virgil refers to two of the great Panhellenic festivals held in Greece, the Olympian and Nemean games, both held in honor of Zeus. The text names the Alpheus, Olympia's river, and the groves of Molorchus, who was host to Hercules before the hero killed the Nemean lion and founded the Nemean games. Virgil imagines these games forsaken in favor of the Italian games that he would institute on the banks of the Mincio.

25–36: The scenes on the doors and the marble statues are alive and moving in a fashion reminiscent of Homer's description of Achilles' shield.

These lines also show the scope of Rome's conquests from Britain to India, Asia Minor, and Egypt.

24–25: The text seems to refer to a stage that could be turned to show a different set. The raising of the curtain signaled the end of a play, for it then concealed the set.

27: The text names *Gangari,* the Ganges, which is meant as a reference to the East in general. The text also has *uictorisque arma Quirini,* "arms of conquering Quirinus." Quirinus was an indigenous god identified with the deified Romulus and also with Mars. Virgil clearly here suggests the prowess of Octavian, who had considered taking the name Romulus.

30–31: The text names *Niphates,* a branch of the Taurus mountain range in Armenia. It also presents the Parthians, inhabitants of what is now northern Iran and southern Turkmenistan, as ineffective warriors. In fact, they were not. In 54 B.C., Crassus, a member of the First Triumvirate with Pompey and Julius Caesar, was governor of Syria. The next year he made an unauthorized incursion on the Parthians, who trounced him and seized his military standards. At the time Virgil wrote the *Georgics,* the standards had not yet been returned, an event that did not take place until 20 B.C. Virgil seems to be expressing hope that Octavian will soon rectify matters.

32–33: Virgil refers here to no conquests in particular but rather expresses his conviction that Rome will prevail on both the eastern and western fronts.

34–36: The text reads *Assaraci proles demissaeque ah Ioue gentis nomina, Trosque parens et Troiae Cynthius auctor,* "the descendants of Assaracus and the names of the nation sent down by Jove and the ancestor Tros and Cynthius, Troy's builder." Tros, who gave his name to Troy, was a great-grandson of Zeus. He in turn fathered Assaracus, who became the grandfather of Aeneas's father Anchises. Cynthius, an epithet of Apollo, refers to Mount Cynthus on Delos, where Apollo and his sister Artemis (the Roman Diana) were born.

37–39: Envy is not a statue in the temple but rather names those who helplessly envy Octavian and his achievements. "Hell's wailing river" is the Cocytus. Ixion, father of Pholus, mentioned in note to II.455–57, was strapped to an eternally revolving wheel because he had attempted to seduce Hera, the wife of Zeus. "The stone that always rolls back down" is that pushed uphill time and again in Hades by Sisyphus, who failed too often to keep his promises to the gods.

40–41: Acknowledging the role of his patron, Maecenas, Virgil returns to the work at hand — completing the *Georgics.*

43–45: The text names Cithaeron, a mountain in southern Boeotia that was associated with the Muses and the worship of Bacchus. It also refers to

Taygetique canes, "dogs of the Taygetus," a mountain range in Sparta famous for its hunting hounds. The text names Epidaurus, a city not suited to horse breeding but located in the definitely horse-worthy Argolis.

48: The text gives the name of "Dawn's consort": Tithonus,

49–94: Virgil instructs on the selection of livestock. Lines 49–71 focus on cattle; lines 72–94, on horses.

53: The look of the cow described here by Virgil may be seen in pictures of nineteenth-century European and American cows. It is only in the past 150 years that cows in the Western world have lost their enormous dewlaps through selective breeding programs.

66–68: In a seemingly sudden shift, Virgil leaves livestock to acknowledge human mortality. The lines may be read as a metaphor for the failure of hard work and as a foreshadowing of the book's last fifth, a bleak account of animal disease and human suffering.

89: The stallion Cyllarus was given to Castor and his brother, Pollux, by Juno, who had received the horse from Neptune.

91: The horses of Mars and those of Achilles are clearly horses used in warfare. The names of the horses in Achilles' team, though not given by Virgil, are Xanthus and Balius.

92–94: Virgil here appropriates the Greek myth of Rhea catching her husband, the pre-Olympian Cronus, with the ocean nymph Philyra. On being discovered in flagrante, he jumped from the bed as a horse and ran away.

95–122: Virgil deals in these lines with various matters pertaining to horses: treatment of the old and the assessment and training of the young, particularly for racing.

99: The "flash fire" of aged sexuality foreshadows the real fire of lust portrayed in line 244 and the fire of disease in line 566.

113: "Vulcan's regal son," named in the text, is Ericthonius, king of Athens.

115: The text reads *Pelethronii Lapithae,* "Lapiths of Pelethronium," a place thought to be in Thessaly. For the Lapiths, see note to II.455–57.

122: The horse was supposedly created when Neptune struck his trident on a patch of earth.

123–37: These lines deal with preparing stallions and mares for successful mating.

138–56: In these lines, Virgil treats of care for both impregnated mares and cows; he also warns about the gadfly, a particular affliction of cattle.

146–47: The text names the river *Silarus,* the modern Sele, located in present-day Campania, which was Lucania in Roman times, and *Alburnus,* a mountain in Roman Lucania.

148–49: The Latin name for the gadfly is *asilus,* a word that echoes the sound of *Silarus.*

151: The river *Tanager* is named in the text. It is thought to be the modern Negro in what was then Lucania.

152–53: The text names *Inachia,* "daughter of Inachus," formally known as Io, a priestess. Once upon a time out of time, Jupiter seduced her. When Juno discovered the affair, he transformed his paramour into a heifer. At that, Juno set a gadfly upon the unfortunate animal, who ran through Egypt and the near East in an unsuccessful attempt to evade the stings. Aeschylus tells the full story in his tragedy *Suppliants.*

157–78: This section describes the care of calves and methods of training them for work as they mature.

179–208: The care and training of young horses, especially for racing and war, are here described.

180–81: "Pisa's Olympian waters" are *Alphea flumina Pisae,* the "Alphean waters of Pisa." The river Alpheus flows through Olympia, site of one of the great Greek athletic festivals, and Jupiter's wild olive grove is found there, as well. Virgil envisions Pisa offering games as important as any in Greece. See note to III.19.

196–97: The text refers to *Hyperboreis Aquilo,* "North Wind from Hyperborean realms." The Hyperboreans were a fabled people said to live in the polar north. It also names Scythia, the ancient country lying north of the Caspian Sea, as a source of storms.

202: The text reads *Elei metus,* "the race-course markers of Elis," a roundabout way of referring to Olympia, which was located in the state of Elis.

204: The text specifies a Belgian war chariot. The Belgae were a people living in the northern part of Gaul.

209–41: Here Virgil illustrates the destruction wrought by sexual rivalry with the tale of two bulls competing for a heifer. The moral is that the energy wasted in combat would be better put to procreation.

219: The text places the heifer on Sila, a mountain in Bruttium (present-day Calabria), the toe of Italy's boot.

242–83: These lines are probably the most famous in the entire poem. Every creature on earth is subject to the irresistible summons of passion. From fish, livestock, and birds to wild animals and humankind, no living animal is exempt from sexual love's erosion of good sense. The section concludes with commentary on the "notable passion of mares" and their impregnation by the West Wind.

258: The text does not name Leander, who swam the Hellespont nightly to visit his beloved Hero, but refers to him simply as *iuuenis,* "the young man."

264: Myth has it that after Bacchus had discovered viticulture and wine making, Juno drove him mad and sent him wandering through the East as far as

India. The goddess Rhea, Juno's mother, restored his sanity, and he returned to Greece. It is said that the chariot bearing him homeward was drawn by lynxes and tigers.

267–68: The text is more specific, mentioning the mares of Potniae that killed their master, Glaucus. Glaucus, a son of Sisyphus, kept mares for racing at his stables in Potniae. Venus caused them to attack and kill him as a punishment because he had refrained from breeding them in order to preserve their strength.

269–70: The text names Gargara, a peak in the Ida range in Crete, and Ascanius, a river that flows into the Black Sea.

280–82: "Mare-madness" is *hippomanes*. When a mare comes into heat, a viscous creamy fluid is indeed expelled from her vulva, and she may flick it off with a swish of her rump.

284–94: These lines comprise the book's second proem, a turning from large domestic herd animals to sheep and goats.

293: The text names Castalia, a spring sacred to the Muses.

294: Addressing the Roman goddess whose special province is flocks of sheep, the text reads *ueranda Pales,* revered Pales.

295–321: This portion of book III surveys the care and feeding of sheep and goats in winter and spring.

299: Virgil here emphasizes the threat posed to livestock by extremes of heat and cold, as he does again at III.441–44. He couldn't have known, however, that lumpy wool and a dermatitis called strawberry foot-rot are caused by a single bacterium, which is not contagious but attacks when sheep are exposed to prolonged damp and injuries to the skin. But, contrary to Virgil's pronouncements, these ailments are not exacerbated by sultry heat and bitter cold.

303–4: Aquarius, the Water-Bearer, sets in late February, at the time of the Roman new year.

306: The text reads *Milesia uellera,* "Milesian wool," referring to the soft, fine wool for which Miletus in southwestern Anatolia was noted.

322–38: These lines treat joyfully of the summertime care of sheep and goats.

339–83: These two portions of book III go far afield to contrast the practices of nomadic Libyan herdsmen to those of settled Scythian shepherds. The Scythians are described at greater length as a counterpoint to the Italians and their mode of agriculture. Neither the Libyans nor the Scythians engaged in regular farming. Virgil also presents extremes of temperature — the eternal summer of Libya, the everlasting winter of Scythia.

345: The text reads *Amyclaeumque canem Cressamque pharetram,* "Spartan dog and Cretan quiver." It is not possible to know why Virgil equipped a Libyan herdsman with such unobtainable objects. But he clearly describes a pastoral way of life without the hard work that Italians expected of themselves.

349–50: The text reads *Maeotis,* an ancient name for the Sea of Azov, and *Hister,* the Roman name for the lower part of the Danube. See note to II.497.

351: Rhodope, a Thracian mountain range, is named in the text. See note to I.332.

355: The measurement given is *septem ulna,* "seven ells," an ell being the length of an arm. So, seven ells equal about twelve feet. Another meaning for *ulna* is "elbow."

372: The text speaks of *punicea formido,* "a rope strung with scarlet feathers to scare game." The rope was stretched out at woods' edge to force deer back into the forest.

384–93: This short section reviews methods of assuring that sheep yield wool of the highest quality.

391–93: This mythical seduction occurs only in the *Georgics,* although it is probably not Virgil's invention. There is debate about whether Pan turned himself into a ram with handsome white wool or simply used a snowy fleece as an enticement. No matter, for the tale is a delightful conclusion to the passage.

394–403: The lines deal with ensuring a supply of goats' milk and producing cheese.

404–13: Nor should the care of dogs be neglected, for they serve well at guarding against thieves and wolves and at hunting wild game.

414–39: This portion of book III identifies troublesome, poisonous snakes as well as giving advice on getting rid of or avoiding them. The passage serves as a transition between the unclouded advice given in the book until now and the darkness of disease that follows. The snakes in themselves represent a serious threat to the success of hard work.

440–77: Virgil discusses the causes, symptoms, and treatment of disease. Straightforward teaching soon yields, however, to an account of "a host of plagues" and the lifelessness they wreak on landscapes everywhere.

441–42: See note to III.299.

449–51: Virgil invented this ointment that compounds olive oil with silver slag, sulphur, pitch, wax, squill, hellebore, and bitumen. Recipes for similar, though less complex, ointments are mentioned, along with the proportions of ingredients, in Latin prose treatises on farming.

461–63: The text names the Bisaltae, a people of Macedonia; Gelonus, a member of the Geloni, a people of Scythia; Rhodope, a mountain range in Thrace; and the Getae, a people living along the lower Danube.

475–76: The text names Noricum, an Alpine territory south of the Danube in what is now Austria; the Iapides, a people living in Illyria on the Adriatic Sea; and the Timauus, modern Timavo, which flows into the Gulf of Trieste.

478–566: The concluding portion of book III deals with plague and its ramifications. Both domestic and wild animals succumb to disease. Special attention is given to the sicknesses of the horse, lines 498–514, and the ox, lines 515–30. Nor is humankind immune but also suffers and dies horribly. Hard work and piety have not prevailed. In an unlooked for, bitter return to the golden Saturnian age, farming ceases.

527–28: The text reads *Massica Bacchi munera,* "Bacchus's Massic gifts." See note to II.143.

551: The text reads *Phillyrides Chiron Amythaoniusque Melampus,* "Phillyra's son Chiron and Melampus, son of Amythaonius." The centaur Chiron, fathered by Cronus, taught Asclepius the arts of medicine. Melampus, a Greek from the Peloponnese, was supposedly the first human being to serve as a physician and to be granted the god-given gift of prophecy.

BOOK FOUR

Bees buzz, fly, and swarm through the *Georgics'* fourth book. The first three-fifths of the book, lines 8–314, center on the natural history of bees. Their communal nature is not only noted time and again but also frequently compared and conflated with an ideal human society. Above all, for the benefit of the whole hive, bees are unceasingly industrious, engaging in the kind of hard work that characterizes human success. The last portion, lines 315–558, contains a narrative mini-epic, technically known as an epyllion, that relates the story of Aristaeus, who has lost his bees to sickness and hunger and seeks to know why. Virgil, of course, supplies the answer.

1–7: The proem, in which Maecenas is addressed.

1: Aristotle, among ancient others, believed that, though bees made wax, honey fell from the sky into the hives. Virgil knew better. He does not echo Aristotelian belief but rather associates bees and their sweet product with sky-dwelling deity. See lines 150–52.

8–50: These lines focus on finding a suitable location for beehives and on the materials from which the hives are made. Both men and bees share in constructing the latter's abodes.

14: Throughout, the bees are identified with small livestock and also humanized, being portrayed as living in stables, houses, chambers, castles, cities, towns, and kingdoms.

15: Virgil summons the story of Procne. Once upon a mythic time, Tereus, king of Daulis in Thrace, married Procne, who bore his son Itys. Tereus, however, fell in love with Procne's sister Philomela. Telling Philomela that Procne had died, he locked his wife away, after cutting out her tongue. But she managed to communicate her plight to Philomela by weaving a message into a tapestry. On release, Procne killed her son and served him up to her faithless husband, who then took up an axe and pursued the sisters as they fled. As he was about to strike them, the gods changed all three into birds: Tereus became a hawk, Philomela a nightingale, and Procne a swallow, her breast forever stained by her crime.

21: Classical naturalists widely believed that the queen bee was male. We do not know if Virgil knew the truth, but even if he did, it would not have been in his best interest to say so, given the poem's emphasis on male accomplishments, especially those of Octavian.

33: This is the only place in book IV in which beehives — *aluaria* — are mentioned. The poem's only other reference to hives is found at II.453.

35–36: Just as other animals are harmed by extreme cold and heat, so is the world of bees. See III.299 and III.441–44.

41: The text reads *munera gluten et visco et Phrygiae seruant pice lentius Idea*, "they keep a store of glue more adhesive than birdlime or the pitch of Phrygian Ida." The mention of Phrygia places Ida and its pitch in Anatolia. Mount Ida actually rises in ancient Mysia, located in the northeastern corner of present-day Turkey.

51–66: This joyful passage sings of winter's retreat and the return of warmth. Then the bees emerge from their homes and become active, gathering pollen, making honey, swarming.

63–64: Some ancient writers believed that loud noises made bees come together, perhaps because they were attracted to the noise or because they huddled out of fear. The Great Mother, *Mater* in the text, is Cybele, whose worship involved cymbals.

67–87: The bees swarm, an event that Virgil describes vividly as a battle between opposing kings. Again, the bees are humanized. The imagery suggests civil war, a situation with which Virgil was all too familiar.

71–72: With martial images, Virgil exaggerates the droning buzz of the bees by comparing it to "hoarse-resonating brass" and "the broken blurting of trumpets."

86–87: Enter the beekeeper, able to calm the swarming bees.

88–102: This portion of book IV deals with distinguishing between superior and inferior species of bees and selecting only the best, while killing the others. The king to be chosen wears regal gold; the lesser king is "uncouth" and drags his "drooping belly." Likewise, the commoners either shine or look "rough and ugly."

103–15: Virgil describes two methods of keeping the bees near their "houses." First, the king may be immobilized by having his wings torn off. Second, the beekeeper can provide his charges with gardens filled with bee-enticing plants.

110–11: Priapus, the son of Aphrodite and Dionysus, was a garden deity who carried a pruning hook. Ithyphallic wooden statues of him were often placed in Roman gardens as a sort of ancient equivalent to a garden gnome. Though the Hellespont may seem far afield, Priapus was originally worshiped there.

116–48: Virgil writes about wild plants and those in domestic gardens; he also tells the tale of the old man of Taranto. The old man may seem at first to be living in golden Saturnian times, but it soon becomes clear he has achieved notable success through hard work.

119: Paestum, located near Naples, was famed for its rose gardens. The claim that the gardens bloomed twice a year is a fiction, like that in II.150, which states that cows bear calves twice yearly and fruit trees twice yield fruit.

125–26: The text reads *sub Oebaliae memini me turribus arcis, cum niger umectat flauentia culta Galaesus,Corycium uidisse senem,* "I remember that under the Oebalian fortress-towers, where the black Galaesus waters golden wheat fields, I saw an old Corycian man." "Oebalian fortress-towers" is an epithet for Tarentum, present-day Taranto. Oebalus was a king of Sparta whose subjects founded the city. The ancient Galaesus is now the Galeno. Corycia was a town in Cilicia, located in what is now southeastern Turkey.

128–29: Crops, grapevines, livestock—the subjects of books I, II, and III are recapitulated, although the old man's land is not suited to such uses.

130–46: Nonetheless, he has enough land for a vegetable patch, fruit trees, and bees. Intensive agriculture is not the only way in which small farming may be accomplished.

149–96: This portion of book IV treats of bees' "natural endowments" and their hard work on behalf of their community. It is a world of all-for-one and one-for-all.

150–2: Bees were not part of the Saturnian golden age but rather a creation of the age of Jupiter. Myth has it that Jupiter's father, Saturn, swallowed his children at birth because it had been prophesied that one of them would dethrone him. But with the Cretans clashing cymbals to mask his cries, the newborn Jupiter was hidden away in a cave in Crete's Mount Dicte. There he was nourished on honey and as a reward gave bees their nature, which was characterized by work.

158–68: Virgil outlines the duties assigned to the groups of bees within the community.

160: Though both Greeks and Romans referred to the nectar of flowers as tears, Virgil may well have intended to nudge the listener to think of Narcissus weeping over his own reflection.

177: The honey made by the bees on Athens's Mount Hymettus was famous in ancient times.

180: Bees do not stay out late at night but bed down at dusk, a fact that Virgil surely knew. Here, however, he uses this fiction to emphasize the preeminence of labor in the bees' world.

195–96: Nor do bees lift and carry pebbles. Aristotle, however, said so, and Virgil took him at his word. No matter; the lines point to the bees' frailty and tininess.

197–209: These lines survey the reproduction and life expectancy of bees. The naturalists of the classical world had various theories about apian reproduction. Virgil chooses to believe that, unlike all other animals, bees do not mate but gather their young from leaves and grass. Another theory of spontaneous reproduction will occur later in this book, in lines 299–314 and 550–58. Passion in bees is directed toward the labor of making honey.

210–18: These lines laud the reverence that the bees show to their king, a reverence greater than that shown by inhabitants of eastern countries to their rulers.

210: The reference to Egypt may be intended to remind listeners of Octavian's defeat of Antony two years before the poem was published.

210–11: The text reads *nec populi Parthorum aut Medus Hydaspes,* "not the Parthian people nor Median Hydaspes." Parthia lay east of the Caspian in part of present-day Afghanistan, Turkmenistan, and Uzbekistan. The Medes' Hydaspes river, the modern Behut, is a tributary of the Indus, which flows through present-day Pakistan.

219–27: Here, Virgil writes lyrically about the bees' immortality. But he distances himself from the topic by writing that "some say" that bees share in the divine soul. The notion may be nothing more than a rumor.

221: Ether, *aether* in Latin, was thought to be the lightest of the elements, so rising above all else to enclose the universe and nourish the stars.

228–250: This portion of book IV deals with how and when to gather honey and lists the pests, from newts to spiders, that may attack the bees and their homes. The mention of the pests leads into the discussion of disease in the subsequent portion.

231: Honey was gathered in the spring and in the fall.

232: The text names Taygete, one of the Pleiades.

234: The text reads *fugiens ubi Piscis aquosi,* "fleeing watery Pisces." No matter that the sun does not actually enter Pisces until February, the Pleiades rise in spring and set in November, a rainy season in Italy.

247: Virgil recalls the myth of Arachne, who challenged Minerva to a weaving contest. Incensed by such arrogance, Minerva turned her into a web-weaving spider.

251–80: Disease attacks the hive. Its progression is like that described for livestock in book III. Advice on remedies is given.

255–56: "Bodies devoid of light" is equivalent to "bodies devoid of life." The language here is that used for human funerals.

268: The Mella is a river that cannot be clearly identified today. Wherever it may be, Virgil clearly chose the name for its resemblance to the Latin words for honey, *mel* and *mellis.*

281–314: But if all the bees should die, despite the remedies, there is one way to replace them: *bugonia.* *Bugonia* is a Greek word meaning "generated by an ox or a bull." Virgil uses this notion of spontaneous generation to frame the last part of book IV. As Virgil surely knew, *bugonia* was indeed a notion, not a fact. He sets its practice at a distance in Egypt. It will reappear in lines 538–58.

283: The "Arcadian master" is Aristaeus, shepherd and beekeeper, who will be named at line 317, where his story begins.

287–93: The boundaries of Egypt are given here, though not accurately: Canopus on the north, Persia to the east, India to the south. Virgil sets the source of the Nile in India; its actual location was not known to the Graeco-Roman world.

287: The text reads *Pellaei gens fortunate Canopi,* "the blessed people of Macedonian Canopus." Canopus, a city on a mouth of the Nile near Alexandria, is characterized as Macedonian because the Ptolemaic rulers of Egypt originally came from Macedonia.

292–93: Scholars have generally decided that these lines precede 291.

314: On the Parthians, see note to III.30–31.

315–558: This portion of book IV presents an epyllion — a mini-epic. It tells the story of Aristaeus, who has lost his bees. With the help of his mother, the nymph Cyrene, he captures the seer Proteus and learns the reason for his loss, which is directly connected to Orpheus's loss of his beloved Eurydice. In the end, all works out well for Aristaeus, who replaces his bee population by means of *bugonia.*

317–32: From the depths of his despair, Aristaeus, representing the aspects of agriculture covered by the *Georgics,* bewails his loss to his mother, Cyrene, in her palace beneath the river Peneus.

318: The Peneus is the present-day Piniós, which flows into the Gulf of Salonica.

323: The text names *Thymbraeus Apollo,* "Apollo of Thymbra," a town in the region surrounding the ancient city of Troy. A famous shrine to Apollo was located there. The story of Cyrene's seduction by Apollo and the subsequent birth of Aristaeus is told by Pindar in *Pythian IX,* which honors the winner of the footrace in full armor who was born in Cyrene, the eponymous city located in Libya.

333–86: Cyrene, surrounded by sister nymphs, hears her son's lamentations and summons him to her palace. En route he beholds the sources of a rush of rivers, eight of them, which are listed. When he reaches the palace, he is graciously greeted, wined, dined, and ritually cleansed.

336–45: Seventeen Nymphs are named in the text: Drymo, Xantho, Ligea, Phyllodoce, Nisaea, Spio, Thalia, Cymodoce, Cydippe, Lycorias, Clio, Beroe, Ephyre, Opis, Deiopea, Arethusa, and Clymene. With the exception of Arethusa, who is well known, the names have been transformed into English equivalents. Four names, those of Nisaea, Spio, Thalia, and Cymodoce (Radiant, Sprightly, Festive, and Wave-Catcher), are bracketed because they were in all likelihood not part of this catalogue, for the line giving these names is found as is in the *Aeneid* V.826.

345–46: "Vulcan's futile efforts" may be a reference to the god's inability to keep his wife, Venus, from having affairs.

367–71: The text names the eight rivers as Phasis, Lycus, Enipeus, Tiberinus, Aniena, Hypanis, Caicus, and Eridanus in that order. For the most part, the translation uses modern names. The Rion flows to the Black Sea in present-day Georgia. Lycus, the modern Great Zab River in western Turkey, is given its English equivalent, "Wolf." Enipeus, an ancient name, is a tributary of the Peneus, the present-day Piniós. Tibernius is, of course, the Tiber, and Aniena, the Anio, both in Italy. Hypanis is the Bug, which now serves as the border between Poland and Ukraine. Caicus is the modern Bakir, located in northwestern Turkey. Eridanus, the classical Greek name for the river, is the present-day Po, the longest river in Italy, which rises in the country's northwest and flows east into the Adriatic.

387–414: Cyrene gives her son instructions on how to capture the seer Proteus and make him divulge the reason that the bees succumbed to sickness and hunger. The passage echoes the instructions given to Menelaus by Eidothea in Homer's *Odyssey* 4.351–470, so that he can capture Proteus and learn not only the fate of the other Greeks after the fall of Troy but also his own future.

387: The text refers to *Carpathio Neptuni gurgite,* "Neptune's Carpathian flood." The Carpathian Sea, named for Carpathos, an island that it encompassed, lay between Crete and Rhodes.

415–52: Aristaeus succeeds in capturing Proteus.

453–527: Proteus answers Aristaeus with a song that recounts the reason for the loss of the bees. It is a divine punishment called for by Orpheus. As it happens, Aristaeus attempted to rape Orpheus's wife, Eurydice, and when she fled, she suffered a snakebite that killed her.

461–63: The text names, in this order, Rhodope; Pangaea; Rhesus's land of Mavortia; the Getae; Hebrus; and *Actias Orithyia,* "Orithyia of Actium."

The first two are mountain ranges in Thrace. Mavortia means "belonging to Mars" and by extension "war-loving"; Rhesus was a Thracian king who was robbed of his horses and killed before the Trojan war by Diomedes and Ulysses. The Getae were a people living along the lower Danube. The Hebrus flowed through Thrace. Orithyia was an Attic princess who married the North Wind.

508: The text names the river Strymon, present-day Strouma.

509: When Proteus tells Aristaeus that Orpheus sang "this song," it is as if Orpheus were responsible for singing the *Georgics*.

517–18: The text reads *solus Hyperboreas glacies Tanaimque niualem aruaque Riphaeis numquam uiduata pruinis lustrabat,* "alone, bereft, he wandered the frozen Hyperborean realms and the wintry Tanais river and the hoarfrost of the Riphaean range." The Tanais is the present-day Don. For the Hyperborean realms, see note to I.240. For the Riphaean range, see note to III.196–97.

523: The text calls the river *Oeagrius Hebrus,* the "Hebrus River of Oeagrus." Oeagrus was the father of Orpheus and king of Thrace, through which the river flowed.

528–58: On Proteus's abrupt departure, Cyrene comes out of hiding and tells Aristaeus how he must make apologies to the nymphs who, in the depths of their grief for Eurydice, caused the loss of his bees. And she instructs Aristaeus in the bee-generating art of *bugonia*.

559–66: The concluding lines of book IV and of the poem are devoted to praise of Octavian's accomplishments and to a brief recollection of Virgil's "undistinguished efforts."

563: This line contains Virgil's one and only mention of his name in any of his works. The text gives the name of Naples as Parthenope, after a siren who was thought to be buried there.

566: Tityrus inhabits Virgil's first *Eclogue* and sprawls in the shade of a beech in its very first line. Here, he is found under the same tree in the last line of the *Georgics*.

GLOSSARY

Achilles: son of the sea nymph Thetis and the mortal Peleus; hero of the Trojan War.

Adriatic Sea: the part of the Mediterranean between Italy and the Balkan peninsula.

Aegean Sea: the part of the Mediterranean between Greece and Asia Minor.

Aeneas: Trojan survivor of the Trojan War; founder of Rome.

Alps: a segment of a mountain range extending from the Mediterranean coast at the border between France and Italy to the Danube River.

Anatolia: the peninsula of Asia Minor that is now Turkey.

Anio: a major tributary of the Tiber River in central Italy.

Apollo: son of Jupiter and Latona; twin brother to Diana (the Greek Artemis); god of the sun, music, archery, and prophecy.

Aquarius: the Water-bearer, a constellation that is one of the signs of the Zodiac.

Arabia: the large peninsula of southwestern Asia.

Ararat: a mountain in eastern Turkey near the Armenia frontier. See note to III.30.

Arcadia: a mountainous region in southern Greece, in the central part of the Peloponnese.

Arcturus: a huge star of fixed magnitude in the constellation Boötes.

Arethusa: a onetime woodland nymph who became a water nymph when Diana turned her into a fountain so that she could escape the lustful advances of the river Alpheus. Here, she is a prime member of Cyrene's court located beneath a river.

Aristaeus: son of the nymph Cyrene and Apollo. Renowned as a hunter and healer, he was also a skilled farmer, prosperous until his bees died.

Asia Minor: a vast peninsula bounded on the north by the Black Sea, on the south by the Mediterranean, and on the west by the Aegean.

Atlas: a Titan; brother of Prometheus and father of the Pleiades and Hyades. After he and other Titans were defeated in their war against the Olympian gods, Jupiter condemned him to bear the heavens upon his shoulders forever.

Attic: an adjective used to describe something in or near Athens.

Auriga: the Charioteer, a constellation between Perseus and Gemini.

Averno: a lake located in the crater of an extinct volcano west of Naples. In 37 B.C., Agrippa, the Roman statesman, converted the lake into a naval harbor, which was connected to the sea by a canal going through Lake Lucrino.

Bacchus: son of Jupiter and Semele, daughter of the king of Thebes; god of wine.

Balearics: islands, including Majorca, Minorca, and Ibiza, in the Mediterranean west of Spain.

Balkan Plains: an extension into present-day Croatia, Serbia, and Romania of the Great Hungarian Plain.

Bears: the constellations Ursa Major , the Great Bear, and Ursa Minor, the Little Bear.

Black River: the ancient Tanager in Lucania, now thought to be the river Negro.

Black Sea: the ancient Euxine Sea, located between Europe and Asia and connected to the Aegean by the Bosporus, Sea of Marmara, and the Dardanelles.

Body-Relaxer: Bacchus.

Boötes: a constellation containing the bright star Arcturus.

Britons: inhabitants of Britannia, a Roman colony.

Bug: the ancient Hypanis; a tributary of the Vistula rising in western Ukraine.

Caesar: The text mentions two Caesars. One is Octavian, who will become Augustus Caesar (63 B.C.–A.D. 14); see II.170; III.16 and 46–48; IV.560. The other is Gaius Julius Caesar (100–44 B.C.); see I.466.

Caicus: the ancient name of the present-day Bakir, located in northwestern Turkey.

Camillus: Marcus Furius Camillus (d. 365 B.C.), aristocrat and statesman, who came to be known as the second founder of Rome after the Gauls sacked the city (ca. 390 B.C.).

Campania: the ancient and modern name of the Italian region in which Naples is located.

Canopus: an ancient city in northern Egypt east of Alexandria; modern name Abukir.

Capua: an ancient city in Campania north of Naples; located near present-day Capua.

Caspian Sea: the world's largest inland sea, with present-day Russia on the northwest, Azerbaijan on the southwest, Iran on the south, Turkmenistan on the southeast, and Kazakhstan on the northeast. In Virgil's day those countries were inhabited by many peoples, including the Medes and Geloni.

Centaurs: creatures with the bodies of men from head to loins and bodies of horses for the rest, complete with hooves and tails. See *Lapiths* and also note to II.455–7.

Cerberus: the three-headed dog that guarded the gates of Hades.

Ceres: daughter of Saturn and Rhea; mother of Proserpina; goddess of agriculture.

Chaos: a "confused and shapeless mass," according to *The Age of Fable* by Thomas Bulfinch, from which Earth and Heaven sprang. They engendered Saturn and Rhea.

China: the land inhabited by the Seres, a people who produced silk.

Chios: an Aegean island, still bearing its ancient name, located near the coast of present-day Turkey.

Chiron: a Centaur renowned for his skill in medicine, hunting, music, and prophesy; he was the teacher of Hercules and Achilles.

Cocytus: one of the five rivers of Hades.

Colchis: an ancient country located at the eastern end of the Black Sea.

Como: a lake located in northern Italy.

Corona: Corona Borealis, the Northern Crown, a constellation between Hercules and Boötes.

Cretan Star: the star of Knossos on Crete; it is an epithet for Ariadne, who was transformed at death into the brightest star in the constellation Corona Borealis.

Crete: a large island in the eastern Mediterranean; legendary home of King Minos and the Minotaur.

Cyclades: islands in the southern Aegean.

Cyclopes: one-eyed giants born of Earth in her experimental days; master builders and smiths, whom Vulcan put to work at manufacturing thunderbolts for Jupiter.

Cyllarus: a horse given to Castor and Pollux by Juno, who had received it from Neptune.

Cyrene: a nymph, mother of Aristaeus, who was fathered by Apollo.

Danube: the modern name for Virgil's Hister, a river flowing into the Black Sea.

Decii: a family, two of whose sons, in the third century B.C., sacrificed themselves in battle to assure victory for their comrades.

Delos: the island in the Cyclades on which Latona gave birth to Apollo and Artemis (Roman Diana).

Dog Star: Sirius.

Don: the modern name for Virgil's Taneis, which flows into the Sea of Azov.

Draco: the Dragon, a constellation.

Dryads: tree nymphs.

Elysian Fields: the place to which the blessed go after death.

Enipeus: a tributary of the river Peneus, modern Piniós.

Epidaurus: an ancient town situated in Argolis in the northeastern Peloponnese.

Epirus: a district on the Ionian Sea in northwestern Greece.

Etna: a volcano in northeastern Sicily.

Etruria: an ancient country occupying much of modern Tuscany and some of Umbria.

Euphrates: a river rising in present-day eastern Turkey and flowing east to join the Tigris near present-day Baghdad.

Eurydice: wife of Orpheus, who tried to bring her back from Hades after she died.

Father of Wine-Making: Bacchus.

First Wine-Maker: Bacchus.

Forum: the center of judicial and public business in Rome.

Furies: three goddesses, Alecto, Megaera, and Tisiphone, who punished people who had not otherwise been brought to justice.

Galeno: the modern name for the Galaesus, a river that flows near ancient Tarentum, now Taranto.

Ganges: a river in northern India.

Garda: a lake in northern Italy between Lombardy and the Veneto that drains into the Po.

Germany: anciently, a region in Europe east of the Rhine and north of the Danube.

Glaucus: a sea god, once a human fisherman.

Goddess of Shepherds: the Italian goddess Pales.

Great Bear: the constellation Ursa Major.

Great Mother: the goddess Cybele, whom Virgil simply styles *Mater,* "Mother."

Hebrus: a river in ancient Thrace, now the Maritsa in Bulgaria.

Helicon: a mountain located in Boeotia and sacred to Apollo and the Muses.

Hellespont: the present-day Dardanelles.

Hercules: the hero, a son of Jupiter, who performed twelve labors in expiation for crimes committed while he suffered a bout of madness.

Hesiod: Greek poet (flourished about 800 B.C.), who wrote *Works and Days,* a didactic poem on farming.

Hyades: Atlas's daughters, who form a V-shaped cluster of stars in the head of the constellation Taurus. They were anciently thought to signal rainy weather when they rose with the sun.

India: an anciently ill-defined region more or less in the area of present-day India but sometimes confused with Arabia.

Indus: a river flowing through Pakistan into the Arabian Sea.

Io: a princess amorously pursued by Jupiter and turned into a heifer by Juno to thwart her husband's lust.

Ionian Sea: an arm of the Mediterranean between southeastern Italy and western Greece.

Ixion: a Lapith who evaded punishment for severe misbehavior until he tried to seduce Juno, whereupon Jupiter had him bound to an ever-revolving, fiery wheel.

Jove: also known as Jupiter, the chief Roman god, presiding over the sky, weather, and affairs of state; husband of Juno.

Judea: the southwestern part of ancient Palestine.

Juno: goddess of heaven, women, and marriage; wife of Jupiter.

Jupiter: see *Jove,* above.

Justice: Iustitia, eponymous goddess of Justice.

Lapiths: a Thessalian people whose king, Pirithous, invited various deities and creatures like the Centaurs to his wedding. There, the Centaurs became riotously drunk and disorderly, and one attempted to rape the bride. This event signaled the beginning of protracted warfare between the Lapiths and the Centaurs. See *Centaurs* and note to II.455–57.

Latona: mother of Apollo and Diana, who were fathered by Jupiter.

Leander: a young man who lived on the Asian side of the Hellespont; he fell in love with Hero, a priestess of Venus, living on the European side. Nightly, guided by a torch that she held, he would swim the mile-wide strait to visit her—until the night that a savage storm arose and drowned him as he attempted the crossing. When his body washed ashore, Hero committed suicide.

Lesbos: an Aegean island off the northwest coast of Turkey.

Libra: the Scales, a zodiacal constellation situated between Virgo and Scorpio.

Libya: in Virgil's day, a general term for all of North Africa.

Lucania: a region of southern Italy on the Gulf of Tarentum—present-day Basilicata on the Gulf of Taranto.

Lucrino: a lake through which a canal was dug in 37 B.C. to connect Lake Averno to the sea.

Lydia: an ancient country in Asia Minor that was bordered on the west by the Aegean Sea. It included the islands of Chios and Samos.

Macedonia: a kingdom in the Balkan peninsula of northeastern Greece

Maecenas: Gaius Maecenas (ca. 70–8 B.C.), minister to Octavian and Virgil's patron.

Maia: one of the Pleiades, daughter of Atlas and mother of Mercury by Jupiter.

Mantua: Virgil's native town located in present-day Lombardy.

Marius: Gaius Marius (ca. 157–86 B.C.), Roman general, six times consul, who achieved notable victories in North Africa and against invading Germanic tribes.

Mars: god of war, son of Jupiter and Juno.

Melampus: the first human being to be divinely granted the power to prophesy, to practice medicine, and to add water to wine.

Melicertes: son of Ino, a princess of Thebes. He was deified by Jupiter.

Mella: a river, perhaps a subtributary of the Po, perhaps imaginary. See note to IV.278.

Mercury: the messenger of the gods; son of Maia and Jupiter.

Mincio: the ancient Mincius, the river of Virgil's hometown, Mantua.

Minerva: goddess of wisdom, born from Jupiter's head.

Molossian Hounds: hunting dogs bred by the Molossi, a people living in central Epirus.

Mount Athos: a mountain on the Chalcidice peninsula in northeastern Greece.

Mount Dicte: a mountain in eastern Crete where Jupiter was reared.

Mount Etna: a volcano in northeastern Sicily.

Mount Ida: a mountain southeast of ancient Troy in Asia Minor, the site at which the Trojan prince Paris awarded the golden apple to Venus for her beauty, received Helen as his reward, and so started the Trojan War.

Mount Parnassus: a mountain in central Greece that was sacred to Apollo and the Muses.

Muses: the nine daughters of Jupiter and Mnemosyne (Memory) who presided over the arts.

Mycenae: an ancient city located in southern Greece in the northeastern part of the Peloponnese; home to Agamemnon and Clytemnestra.

Naples: a city in Campania, located on the west coast of central Italy.

Nemea: a location in the northeastern Peloponnese at which Hercules slew the Nemean lion and the Nemean games, one of the great Panhellenic athletic festivals, were held.

Neptune: brother of Jupiter, god of the ocean.

Nereus: a water deity who fathered the Nereids, including Thetis, the mother of Achilles.

Olympia: a plain in southern Greece in the northwest part of the Peloponnese. It was the site of the Olympian games held in honor of Jupiter.

Olympus: a mountain located in northeastern Greece in Thessaly; the home of the Olympian pantheon.

Orpheus: son of a Thracian king and the Muse Calliope, a great poet and musician, whose music enchanted wild beasts and caused the trees to dance.

Ossa: a mountain located in Thessaly in northeastern Greece.

Paestum: an ancient town in Lucania on the Gulf of Paestum (modern Gulf of Salerno), famous for its rose gardens.

Pallene: one of the three promontories of the Chalcidice peninsula in northeastern Greece.

Pan: god of flocks and herds, shepherds, and beehives.

Panopea: one of the Nereids, daughters of Nereus.

Parthians: inhabitants of Parthia, a country occupying some of present-day Iran and Turkmenistan. See note to III.30–31.

Peace: the Roman goddess Pax.

Pelion: a mountain located to the southeast of Mount Ossa in Thessaly in northeastern Greece.

Peloponnesus: the very large peninsula forming the southern part of Greece.

Pelops: son of King Tantalus and a bosom companion of Jupiter until, lacking enough food for a banquet, the king cooked Pelops and served him up. But only one goddess, Vesta, ate a bite from the boy's left shoulder. Later, his life restored, she gave him an ivory shoulder to replace the one she'd gnawed.

Peneus: a Thessalian river flowing through the Tempe Valley into the Gulf of Salonica.

Persia: ancient Media, a land that occupied part of present-day Iran.

Philippi: a town in eastern Macedonia, where, in 42 B.C., Octavian, later to become Augustus Caesar, and Mark Antony defeated Crassus and Brutus, the main assassins of Julius Caesar.

Phrygia: an ancient country located in central Asia Minor.

Pisa: a city located in ancient Etruria (modern Tuscany).

Planter God: an Italian god of vegetation, later identified with Bacchus.

Pleiades: daughters of Atlas, companions of Diana, who were changed into doves by the gods and later set as stars in the heavens amid the constellation Taurus.

Po: a northern Italian river with delta of several mouths flowing into the Adriatic Sea.

Pollux: son of Leda and Jupiter, who became a swan to inseminate her. Pollux, his brother Castor, and Helen, later known as Helen of Troy, were hatched from an egg.

Priapus: son of Venus and Bacchus; he is a gardener who carries a large pruning hook.

Procne: a Thracian queen turned into a swallow. See note to IV.15.

Prometheus: a Titan, brother to Atlas and Epimetheus, who brought fire to humankind.

Proserpina: daughter of Ceres, who married Pluto, god of the lower world, and so became queen of the dead.

Proteus: a son of Neptune and a water deity renowned for wisdom, prophecy, and an ability to change his shape at will.

Remus: twin brother of Romulus, cofounder of Rome.

Rhesus: a Thracian king, ally of Troy's King Priam; he was killed by Ulysses.

Rhodes: a large Greek island located in the southeastern Aegean Sea.

Rion: modern name of the ancient Phasis river, which flows to the Black Sea.

Rome: Italy's major city, located on the Tiber in the region of Latium.

Romulus: twin brother of Remus, cofounder of Rome.

Sabines: an ancient people living to the northeast of Rome.

Saturn: a Titan, son of Earth and Heaven; husband of Rhea; father of Jupiter and Ceres.

Scipios: Scipio Africanus the Elder (236–184/183 B.C.), who defeated the Carthaginian general Hannibal in 202 B.C., and Scipio Africanus the Younger (185/184–129 B.C.), famed for his accomplishments in the Third Punic War, 148–146 B.C., and the conquest of Spain, 134–133 B.C.

Scorpio: the Scorpion, a zodiacal constellation.

Scythia: an ancient country north and northeast of the Black Sea.

Sea of Azov: a gulf of the Black Sea connected to the sea by a strait.

Sele: the ancient river Silarus, located in the Roman region of Lucania, present-day Campania.

Sicily: an Italian island located in the Mediterranean south of the Italian mainland.

Silvanus: an Italian god associated with woodlands and uncultivated land.

Sparta: an ancient Greek city, also known as Lacedaemon, located in the Peloponnese.

Styx: the prime river of Hades' five rivers.

Taranto: ancient Tarentum, located on the Gulf of Taranto, an arm of the Ionian Sea.

Taurus: the Bull, a zodiacal constellation that contains the Pleiades and Hyades.

Tempe: the Thessalian valley through which the river Peneus flows into the Gulf of Salonica.

Theseus: the Greek hero who, among other feats, slew the Minotaur.

Thessaly: a region located in northeastern Greece south of Macedonia.

Thetis: a Nereid, daughter of Nereus, mother of Achilles.

Thrace: an ancient region located on the Balkan peninsula north of the Aegean Sea.

Tiber: the river flowing through Rome into the Tuscan Sea.

Tisiphone: one of the three Furies.

Titans: giants, born of Heaven and Earth, who ruled the world until overthrown by the gods of the Jovian era.

Tityrus: a Greek personal name used to denote a shepherd.

Tuscan Sea: also known as the Tyrrhenian Sea, the arm of the Mediterranean that stretches along the west coast of Italy.

Tyrian purple: a crimson or purple dye that the Greeks and Romans extracted from mollusks.

Ultima Thule: the most northerly place in the habitable world.

Umbria: a region in central Italy.

Venus: goddess of erotic love who rose from the sea; Vulcan's incurably unfaithful wife.

Vesta: goddess of the hearth and home.

Vesuvius: an Italian volcano located on the Bay of Naples.

Virgo: the Virgin, a zodiacal constellation lying due south of the Big Dipper's handle.

Vulcan: son of Jupiter and Juno, husband to Venus, god of the smithy who was responsible for seeing to it that Jupiter's thunderbolts were duly forged.

War: Mars, son of Jupiter and Juno, god of war.

Wine God: Bacchus.

Zodiac: a heavenly belt divided into twelve constellations that have been used immemorially as signs for planting and harvesting: Aries, Taurus, Gemini, Cancer, Leo, Virgo, Libra, Scorpio, Sagittarius, Capricorn, Aquarius, and Pisces.